COLOR

AND

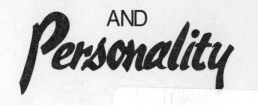

D0769758

AUDREY KARGERE

SAMUEL WEISER, INC.
York Beach, Maine

First published in 1949 by
Philosophical Library, Inc.

First paperback edition (revised) in 1979 by
Samuel Weiser, Inc.
Box 612
York Beach, Maine 03910

Reprinted 1982, 1984, 1986, 1990

ISBN 0-87728-478-4

Cover art ©Jade Photography, 1989

Printed in the United States of America by
Baker Johnson, Inc.

Dedicated to

My beloved Mother and brothers Adolf and Fred and to the memory of my Father and my beloved teacher Dr. Ernest J. Stevens whose faith in me as "The Burbank of the Human Plant," led me onward and upwards towards my goal! To my sincere friend and helper, inspired writer, and poet, Vivian Shaw Kennedy and to all those who have blazed the trail before me sending me this inspiration and light!

FOREWORD

It gives me great joy to know that serious minded thinkers are recognizing the importance of research into the only thing we have in all this universe—for LIGHT is all there is. Light is the least known and most neglected by mankind. It pleased me much to hear Audrey Kargere refer to Light as the universal language.

For years I have been saying that God's language in speaking to man is LIGHT. Light-waves make up His universe. Light-waves are recorded in colors—according to wave-frequencies and pressures. Bodily conditions are affected by these frequencies and pressures. Change the pressures and you change the conditions. This fact is the basis of color-therapy.

WALTER RUSSELL

CONTENTS

PART I

PART II

PREFACE

When I first started out in my field of work as a lecturer, I sat in a train, planning my first address and wondering exactly what I would say. The train tore through the night while I worked determinedly on my notes. The night was black; there was no color or ray of light. Big raindrops splashed against the window pane, making a sorry sound—almost as if God were crying. Morning found me still working. When I arrived at my destination, I noticed a huge placard in a store window, announcing to the world in large black letters that I was going to hold "Color Clinics."

A feeling of despair came over me as I saw this, and for a moment I felt discouraged. Then suddenly I realized that I had pioneer work to do: making the language of color known to those who had never heard it. I stood silently in front of the store window. There was reverence in my soul as I gazed at the placard. A deep responsibility weighed on my shoulders. The universe had taken things in hand, and I was here to give Color Clinics.

A woman stopped by my side and I caught a glimpse of her face. She was reading the sign, anxiously. She looked as though she were searching for something, and when I saw her face light up, I knew that that would be my reward.

I rode up to the auditorium, praying that I might be the instrument through which inspiration might come to those who heard me. A little voice within me seemed to say, "I give my mind, body and soul to the services of my fellow man, so that the mighty creative forces may be felt and better understood in the hearts of men." I stood in front of the crowded auditorium paralyzed with fear. The audience turned to a sea of black.

My memory left me. I could think of nothing that I had planned to say. A glowing introduction was being given as to my accomplishments, and when it was necessary for me to speak I only noticed my dress swaying in front of me, caused by the shaking of my knees. The little voice within me again said, "Why not use the advice that you give others—Gold-mine yourself! Make those powers within you come alive!" Immediately there flashed in front of me the picture of the Christ. He seemed to seat Himself in the audience. I looked directly at Him, and suddenly a surge of power and confidence welled up within me, and I knew what I was going to talk about. "Do you see what I see?" I asked laughingly of my audience. "My knees are shaking, I am so nervous. I think I'll lecture sitting down."

A wave of amusement swept the audience as I seated myself in a chair. That day I learned two things: one was the art of public speaking through gold-mining my audience and making them feel my weaknesses by sharing any small technique that I might have discovered to conquer my faults; the other was having faith in a higher power and, by directing my attention to it, bringing myself in alignment with the higher color bodies—the only fountainhead of inspiration.

The study of color, given in this book, is based on the research findings of scientists and psychologists, going back as far as the days of Egypt, Babylon, India and China. Color as a science, or shall I say a near-science, has been compared in its findings with modern psychology. People's responses have been alike for several thousands of years. It seems as if their associations have also remained the same, regardless of modern progress.

PREFACE

I have lectured extensively throughout the United States, holding Color Clinics, and I direct a studio at Carnegie Hall in New York. I have, therefore, noted the reactions of several thousands of individuals, keeping a record of their case-histories. I have also sent out questionnaires to all my students. The result of all this research and investigation has been added to other historical and scientific evidence. The research of great scientists and investigators, such as Professor Ernest J. Stevens, Luther Burbank, Dinshah Gadiahli, Ivah Bergh Witten, Faber Birren and many others, has helped me in my studies and conclusions. I wish to thank these men for any suggestions that they may have given to me along this path.

> I thought of ourselves
> Why I'm one of ourselves,
> But what sort of selves are we?
> So I walked with myself,
> And I talked with myself,
> And this is what myself said to me:
>
> Oh, you fool of a thing,
> Where are you now,
> Are you tied to yourself and not free?
> Then look at yourself,
> Your real, real self.
> And see where yourself should be!
> *E. J. S.*

AUDREY KARGERE

ON CHROMATIC VISIBLE CHEMICAL REACTIONS

ELEMENT	REACTION	WAVE COLOR
SODIUM &	Digestion, nerve, brain eliminator of CAR-BONIC ACID gas and waste carbon only	YELLOW
CHLROINE*	wholesome in organic form. Keeps the blood from clotting. Keeps gall from thick-	*GREEN
toxic expeller digestive acids	ening. Keeps deposits from forming. Helps form lymph, blood, saliva, pancreatic, juice, bile, emulsifies, supplies fats.	
POTASSIUM	Heals, promotes growth, prevents consti-pation, aids capillarity.	MAGENTA
CALCIUM	Builds bone, prolongs life, strengthens blood cells, combines with protein molecules.	ORANGE
MAGNESIUM	Laxative, promotes sleep, prevents wrinkles, bone, muscle, hormel osmossis.	YELLOW
SILICON	Hair, eyes, skin, lungs, muscles.	ORANGE
COPPER	Promotes seed growth, gland secretions, kidney regulation, blood, sugar.	ORANGE
PHOSPHORUS	Prevents fatigue, builds bone, muscle, brain, nerves, phosphates.	LEMON
SULPHUR	Removes inflamation, disease resistant, combines with Proteins, PURIFIES, CLEANSES, HEALS.	LEMON
FLUORINE	Nourishes, spleen, hair, teeth, skin, nerves, blood magnitism.	TURQUOISE
IODINE	Small amounts for thin people will increase NITROGEN METABOLISM, and aid fattening. 4 spoons a day will reduce fat people. Burns out.	LEMON
ALUMINUM SEED	Glands, kidneys.	ORANGE
ARSENIC	CLEANING.	ORANGE
BROMINE	CLEANSING with iodine aids SILICON. Forms four groups of organic Proteins.	PURPLE

VIBGYOR

(primary)

WAVES

SPLMT
(secondary & tertjarv.)

If you will place green cellophane paper over your face and look at the electric light as you lie in bed, or for that matter, look through the window, the pituitary gland, which is the master gland governing all the other glands of the body, will be stimulated.

R-Red; O-Orange; Y-Yellow; G-Green; B-Blue; V-Violet; (L)-Local Treatment; (G)-General Treatment.

MIND

Anxiety	B-G	(G)
Dullness (Sluggishness)	O-Y	(G)
Irritability	O-Y	(L)
Memory Weak Y (L)	G-Y	(G)

HEAD AND BRAIN

Eruption (dry)	G-Y	(L)
Eruption (moist)	B-G	(L)
Numbness	R-Y	(L)
Pain (general headache)	B	(L)
Pain (congestion)	Y-B	(L)
Perspiration (cold)	G	(G)
Redness (inflamed)	R-B-G	(G)
Redness (bloated)	Y-B	(L)
Shaking	O-G	(L)
Swollen glands	B-G	(G)
Tension	O-Y	(L)
Tired	B-G	(G)
Trembling sensation	O	(G)
Sinus (congestion of cavaties, accompanied by pus)	G-O-V	(L)

NOSE

Sensitive to air	B-G	(L)
Bleeding	B-V	(L)
Catarrh	G-Y	(G)
Crusts	G-Y	(L)
Sneezing	B	(L)
Snuffles	B-G	(L)
Pus in nasal passages R-B-G on kidneys; blue on head.		

STOMACH

Appetite (capricious but knows not for what) G (L)	G-Y	(G)
Appetite (diminished)	O	(L)
Coldness	R	(G)
Emptiness (weak feeling, faintness, goneness, sinking sensation on heart)	G-Y	(G)
Uneasiness	B	(L)
Flatulence	R	(L)
Heartburn	G-Y	(L)
Hiccough, anterior	R	(G)
Hiccough, posterior	Y-B	(G)
Nausea	O	(L)
Pain from diarrhea	B-V	(L)
Pain from constriction	O	(L)
Vomiting (poisoning) R (L)	G	(G)
Vomiting (pregnancy)	B-V	(L)

EYES

Dark around eyes	G-Y	(G)
Itching	B-G	(L)
Pain (after straining)	B	(L)
Pain (inflamation)	B-V	(L)
Conjunctivitis (red inflamation, watery discharge)	V-B	(L)
Conjunctivitis (acute)	V-B	(L)
Iritis (inflamation of iris)	B	(L)
Glaucoma (drainage stoppage)	B-Y	(L)
Weak eyes (general) Spectra		(G)
Cataract (mineral deposit)	B-G	(L)
Retinitis (inflamation of the retina)	B-V	(L)
Myopia (near sight)	B-G	(L)

EARS

Catarrh	G-Y	(G)
Discharge (offensive)	B-G	(G)
Deafness	Y-O	(L)
Eruptions	G-Y	(G)
Pain	B-V	(L)
Suppuration	B-G	(G)

FACE

Cracked Lips	B-G	(L)
Dryness	O	(L)
Swelling (kidneys)	R-G-Y	(G)

MOUTH

Cracked (tongue inflamed)	B-Y	(L)
Detached (gums from teeth)	B	(L)
Taste (wanting)	Y-O	(L)
Taste (bad abdomen) Y (L)	G-Y	(G)

TEETH

Chattering	B-V	(G)
Dwarfed (children's appear late) alternate R-G abdomen	G	(G)
Pyorrhea	O-Y	(G)

EXTERNAL THROAT

Pain	B-V	(L)
Pain (cervical glands)	B-G	(G)
	B-V	(L)
Pulsation	Y-B	(L)
Stiffness of sides	G-Y	(G)
Swelling B-V (L)	G-Y	(L)

RESPIRATION

Accelerated (too)	O	(L)
Arrested	R-Y	(L)
Convulsive	Y-B	(G)
Difficult, from anxiety G (G)	O	(L)
Difficult, from pain	Y-B	(L)
Difficult, gasping for air	B	(G)
Hysterical	Y-B	(G)
Intermittent	B-V-R	(G)
Slow	O	(L)
Obstructed B (L)	G-Y	(G)
Painful	B-G	(L)
Rattling during cough	B-G	(L)
Wheezing (acute)	B-Y	(L)

SKIN

Acne	R-Y	(L)
Acne (pus forming)	O-G	(L)
Boiles, carbuncles-promore to a head with	Y-R	
Heal with	G-O	
Eczema (chronic acne)	B-O-R	(L)
Skin, purulent disorders	B-G	(G)
	V-B	(L)
Ulcer O-Y (G)	B-G	(L)

BLOOD AND DUCTLESS GLANDS

Thrombosis (blood clot formed within circulatory system) R-Y		(G)
Prostatitis (inflamation of the prostate gland)	O-V-B	(L)
Blood (run down & anemic) G 3 to 4 minutes daily R-B on kidneys & genital, 10 minutes, 3 times a week.		
Pituitary (abnormal activity)	V-B-G-Y	(L)
Pernicious anemia V-R over kidneys	Y-G	(G)
Arterio Sclerosis Y-V (L)	O	(L)

NERVES

Sciatica R-V (G)	R-V-B	(L)
Arthritis	O-V-B	(L)
Chorea-St. Vitus Dance	V-O	(G)
Hiccough	B-Y-O	(L)
Neuritis Y-B (G)	G-V	(L)
Locomotor ataxia R-Y (L)	V-G	(G)
Neurosis (a functional disease of the nervous system)	V-R-O	(G)

KIDNEYS AND BLADDER

Inflamation B (L)	B-G	(L)
Pain in kidney region	Y-B	(L)
Urging to urinate (morbid desire) on genitals	B-V	
Urging (constant dribbling) on kidneys G-Y	B	(L)
Urination (irritating in newly married women) on genetalia	G	(L)
Urination, retarded kidneys	R	(L)
Albumin, a protein substance	V-B-G	(G)
Bladder	B-G	(L)
Calculus (kidney stones and gall stones)	V-B-Y	(G)
Dropsy B-R	V-Y	(G)
Uremia on kidneys	V-G-R	
Urine (think) on kidneys R-Y & G-Y (G)		
Suppression of urine	G-Y	(G)

HEART ACTIONS

Accelerated (too)	O	(L)
Arrested (from faintness)	R	(G)
Convulsive	Y-B	(G)
Difficult	B-V-R	(G)
Difficult (from fear)	R	(L)
Intermittent B-V-R	G	(G)
Angina pectoris (a sense of choking or suffocation)	Y-R	(L)
Leakage of heart on spine; Y on bowels	B-V	(L)
Fibrosis (hardening of the arteries) Y-O (L)	V-O-Y	(G)
Fatty heart	V-B-R	(G)
Low Blood pressure	R-O-Y	(G)
High blood pressure	G-B-V	(G)
Palpitation	G-B-V	(G)
Aneurysm (a circumscribed dilation of the walls of an artery) B-G (L)	G	(G)
Pericarditis	R-O-B	(L)

LIVER AND PANCREAS

Abcess of liver	Y-O-B	L&G
Cancer of liver	G-Y-V	(L)
Pancreatitis (inflamation of pancreas) Y-O (L)	B-V	(G)
Jaundice R-O-V-W-Spectra		(G)
Gall stones V-Y (L)	B-W	(G)
Cirrhosis of liver Y-O (L)	V-B	(G)

RECTUM

Hemmorrhage (from anus)	B-V	(L)
Itching	B-G	(L)
Numbness (from anus)	R-Y	(L)
Pain (from piles)	B-V	(L)
Slow action of rectal muscles	O	(L)

CHEST

Asthma	Spectra 10 min.	Y-O-B
Bronchitis (acute)	B-V-R	(L)

ABDOMEN

Colic	o (G)	R	(L)
Cramps		Y-B	(L)
Distention	R-B on kidneys	R-Y	(L)
		G	(G)
Fat		O	(L)
Inflamation		B-G	(L)

Appendicitis. B-V-G White
3 mins. for each color, 1/2 to
3/4 hour's treatment. Repeat
at one hour intervals until relieved.

Cancer	G-F (L)	V-Y	(G)
Constipation		Y-O	(L)
Diarrhea		G-V-B	(L)
Dyspepsia, nervous		Y-R	(L)
Enteritis (inflamation of		B-W	(G)
the intestines)		B-Y-V	(L)
Gastritis (acute or chronic)			
		B-Y-V-O	(L)

Hematemesis (vomiting
blood) B-V with intermediate
flashes of R (L) & B on spine.
Pain, with diarrhea and

bloody stool		B-V	(G)
Intestinal tumor	R-G (L)	V-B	(G)
Obstruction		Y-R	(L)
Peritonitis	B-Y (L)	G-O	(G)
Dysentry	(G)	B-V	(L)

GENERAL

Diabetes	G-Y	(G)
Diphtheria	G-V-B-O	(G)
Exophthalmic goiter	G	(L)
Fat	O	(L)
General Pain	B-Y-W	(G)
General Tonic - Spectra	R-O-Y	(G)
Gangrene	O-G-B	(L)
Head noises (buzzing)	Y-V-B	(L)
Stomach (sluggish)	O-Y	(L)
Indigestion	B-O	(L)
Colitis Bleeding	O-B	(L)
Rupture	G-V-B	(L)
Hay Fever B on head	B-G	(G)
Influenza G-Y (L)	O-V	(G)
Convulsions	Y-R-B	(G)
Spasms	B-V-G	(G)
Malaria	G-O-V	(G)
Measles B-G Spectra		(G)
Mumps	B-W	(G)
Paralysis R-V-O Spectra		(L)
Rheumatic Fever	B-Y-G	(L)

Rheumatism G-Y over bowels
R-V over kidneys; B-G over
left ear

Smallpox	G-B-R	(G)
Superficial pain	R-B	(G)
Tuberculosis G-O (L)	B-R	(G)
Tumor	B-G-Y	(L)

Typhoid (an acute fever)

medication by physician	G-B	(L)

Sleeplessness   G-face. If still
awake, change to blue.
Nervousness   V-B face.

THROAT

Catarrh	B-V-Y	(L)
Whooping Cough	Y-B-V	(L)
Chronic catarrh (mucus		
discharge)	B-G	(L)

TIME

When one color is specified 20 minutes.
Where two colors are specified 10 minutes each.
Where three or more colors are specified 5 minutes each.

NOTE: If the Thyroid gland is too active, you should use all three colors on the
left half of the page, such as Violet, Indigo and Blue -- each of these 20 minutes
in duration, all there is to do is to lay cellophane or colored glass over the part
of the body you wish to treat.

Chapter I

THE HUMAN AURA

If we could all have psychic insight, we would see each human aura aglow with fine ethereal emanations. In fact, we would begin to realize that everything that lives and vibrates, shines forth into the universe. The fluctuation and change of these emanations would charm and interest us beyond all human conception. We would see auras as tranquil as a lake, and as active and excited as roaring flames. We would see radiant emotions of love and the deep dark flashes of anger and hate. Just as the gods of the ancients likened the sun to the rays of God, we would take auras and translate them by their colors. Religions, for many centuries, have had color rites. The nimbus of the saint, for example, is used to inspire spirituality and give meaning to religious teachings. To the ancient Persians the study of the aura was necessary as a mark of distinction of spiritual and mental progress.

Science, today, readily admits the existence of the aura, although it discounts its mystic associations. This occult aspect of astral light shows the great struggle to correlate color with human temperament. Art, no matter how old, verifies the traditions of color science. The meanings·assigned to astral hues are found to be the same,

The primary colors are red, yellow and blue. White is the blending of all hues; black is their absence. All other hues and shades are mixtures.

Red means the physical plane of being; it indicates friendship, love, health and vigor.

1

Yellow represents the intellectual plane of being. Golden yellow is the highest form of intellect.

Blue represents the spiritual and religious plane of being. Dark blue surges from people with great religious feelings, whereas light blue indicates merely devotion to noble ideals.

Orange, product of red and yellow, unifies body and mind. It represents wisdom and justice.

Green, the combination of mind and spirit, distinguishes the lover of nature. Characteristics are sympathy, altruism, charity. Grayish-green is the symbol of jealousy and deceit; Emerald green shows versatility and ingenuity, while pale green means sympathy and compassion.

Purple, red-blue, indicates the union of body and spirit. It is a symbol of the ideal and the sublime. It indicates a love for ceremony.

Black is the negation of all being.

White is pure spirit; the positive pole. It signifies spiritual attainment, perfection.

The colors in the aura are sometimes soft and hazy, while at other times they have spear-like flashes of lightning.

Any indication of black in the aura indicates hatred and malice. Gray means fear and depression.

Anger is shown by red on black backgrounds, whereas sensuality is seen through a maroon shade of red.

A dull brown indicates avarice, whereas a grayish brown shows selfishness, and a greenish brown represents jealousy.

Have you ever considered a human being in the terms of an electric neon sign? Faber Birren has brought out this thought. The aura of a savage or his neon radiation is dull yellow and grayish blue, dull orange, and the brownish red of sensuality. The dull yellow is above his head, whereas the colors give an irregular outline and choppiness to the aura. The civilized person has a much higher radiation. His aura contains more yellow, pure red and clear blue. During emotional storms his aura flashes black and red with anger. When frightened he radiates a gray mist. During moods of devotion he emanates blue.

The aura of the superman is glorious, comparable to a desert sunset and to the softness of a twilight sky. The strongest radiation of yellow surrounds his head.

Chapter II

COLORS; THEIR PHYSICAL EFFECTS

What is one man's meat is another man's poison. This is an old adage, but a true one, especially in the realm of color. The selection of color and its application should be handled with the utmost discretion, since they are often used medicinally. For a great many years medical practitioners have used color therapeutics, especially in the treatment of nervous patients. It also takes its place as a preventive as well as a cure. The mental side of color reacts on the physical side, not only through suggestion, but by vibratory light speeds that result in color.

Therefore, we should become familiar with the actual characteristics of each color if we are to blend them, using a little of this and a little of that. It will then be as easy to combine their natures as it will be to assemble them for their color value, and we will be able to get any desired result.

Red is the color of activity. It is the vibration that we first consider in our study because, as it is really the most attractive color, its influence is both good and bad. It is therefore, necessary to know just how to use this color in order to obtain all of its beneficial effects without reaping evil results. In other words, to be always surrounded by the great force of red might prove to be very disastrous to the ordinary individual.

Dr. Babbitt suggests that maniacal patients who are violent should be placed in a room whose influence is that of blue vibration. If they contact the red ray, they become worse and more violent.

4

Dr. Wade has proved that red excites and makes one emotional. It inspires one to action. Dr. Zeller warns us that red must be administered with the same discretion as morphine and chloroform. It is because of its great stimulation that too much red will often disturb the mental balance of a delicately poised mind.

Jules Guerin, noted color expert of the San Francisco Exposition, has proved beyond doubt that red excites the mind, and Dr. L. E. Landon shows that the ill-proportioned use of red in wallpaper, as well as the use of red draperies, causes nervousness, severe headaches and bad temper.

Because red is an excitant, producing superficial energy which when relieved causes mental outbursts, and when suppressed leads to eye-strain, nervousness and headaches, this color should be used in a restrained way. Many a marital rift comes from too much red in the wallpaper. Also, red acting as a stimulant may produce superficial and abnormal passion which could lead to morbidity or moral degeneracy. It might be labeled the color of indiscretion, passion, sensuality, and it is really due to the recognition of the psychology of color that we have been led to associate certain neighborhoods, where the looseness of morals is rampant, with red.

Color reactions are brought about partly by the association of ideas, which is of course the mental aspect. However, real excitement or depression of the nervous system is often produced by color. It is impossible to sit in a bright red room for any length of time without feeling restless and uncomfortable. In "Color In The Modern Hospital," William O. Ludlow, a New York architect, points out that color produces mental reactions which have immediate physical reflections. Red, for example, has a key that is too high; it overstimulates the nervous system.

The value of the red ray cannot be overlooked. At a meeting of The Medical Association of Canada, the value of the red ray was brought out. One doctor stated that he had experimented with colors in different ways and found that the influence of the red ray would prevent pitting in cases of smallpox. He elaborated on the idea of using the red ray occasionally but not continuously. He stated that when he put the patients in a red room where the walls, ceilings and window glass were equipped with red, including the electric light bulbs, it produced such a reaction on the nervous system that the patients became quarrelsome and began to fight among themselves as well as with the nurses. The doctors themselves became unnerved by the influence of this color agitation, and before long they too were at war with the nurses.

As a result, it was decided that red should only be used in small doses. To substantiate this conclusion, we may note that the lovers of this color, those people who use it exclusively, are usually fiery and quick on the trigger. These people are usually miserable half of the time, repenting for their outbursts.

It was found that when the employees of a film factory called "Lumiere," at Lyons, France, worked all day in a red light vibration, they were lively, and sang and gesticulated. When they switched to a green light, these employees became less tired at night and much more calm.

In the last century, it was customary for dining rooms to be decorated with red walls and pink ceilings. This was considered fashionable. The living rooms were decorated in green to act as a contrast. Then the vogue for red dining rooms went out of fashion and the hall was decorated in red. The living room, however, remained the same. Just about that time German scientists and physicians began to study the effect of color on the physical. They began to experiment on guinea pigs and used the red ray. The result was noteworthy: guinea pigs were more subject to cancerous throats under this ray, and the parts most affected were the digestive organs. As their research continued and they extended their investigation to people, they noticed that the red influence at meal time produced an irritation through fermentation but which came first. The color change or the scientific investigation? They traced it to the red ray which acted on the physical. Therefore, it was quite natural that the red dining room was doomed, never to come back into fashion. This was an instance in which enlightenment dissipated the darkness of ignorance.

From all these experiments, we can say that red is the color of fermentation. It was from the nervous excitations produced by the red environment that the ill effects of food were derived, the bombardment of super-saturated light elements acting on the fermentation of the stomach, causing irritation in the digestive tract and leading to inflammation. Increased glandular secretional activity, caused by the inflammation, furnished the necessary organic elements to keep the ferment in activity. Ulcers were produced through this constant irritation in the stomach, and no cure was effective until the cause was removed. With the exit of the red dining room, however, we come to the end of a period of gastro-intestinal disorders.

Another very interesting effect of color was reported by the Berlin Medical Society of The Charity Hospital concerning "Issiman blue," a dye used by the textile industry for the coloring of cottons and artificial silk. When injected into patients being treated for tumors by X-Ray and radium, this dye, it was stated, caused tumors to dry up or at least to grow smaller.

If you still are not convinced of the effects of color, I would like you to try an experiment designed to show the effect of rays of light of different colors. Take three green tomatoes about the same size, picked from the vines at about the same time and showing the same state of growth. Wrap one of the tomatoes in a white cloth, one in a red cloth, and the third in a black cloth, and place them in the sun to ripen. Do not use glass over the tomatoes for glass will exclude the ultra-violet ray which is so essential to growth.

Remember that all of the tomatoes were in about the same stage of development when you picked them and wrapt them. Now, wait for the remainder of the tomatoes on the vine to ripen. When they do, unwrap the tomatoes you picked green. The one in the white cloth will have ripened to the same degree as the ones on the vines. Cut it open and you will find that it is as ripe as any naturally ripened fruit.

Next take the tomato that is wrapped in the red cloth. Cut it open and you will notice traces of black filament around the seeds and in the pulp. This indicates that the red vibration produced a fermentation during the ripening period, which did not occur in the tomato covered with the white cloth.

Lastly, unwrap the tomato in the black cloth. Lo and behold, you will find that it has not ripened at all, and on cutting it open, you will find that it is withered and decayed!

This clearly indicates that the effect of white light is extremely healthy. The red ray is stimulating and fermentative, whereas the black cloth deprived the fruit of any light or color. Thus black might easily be considered the absence of all color, as its qualities absorb all the rays of white light.

This experiment proves that although the tomato could not sense or see the light, it was nevertheless affected by the different colored rays. Even though we are not conscious of the different colored rays, they still have an effect on us just as much as they affect the vegetable kingdom. Therefore the colors of our home, our dress and our surroundings should be well balanced or eventually we shall suffer the consequences. It will then do us no good to take a pill or a dose of medicine but we will have to seek the cause of our discomfort.

If you are ill, and are sent to the seashore or to the mountains and you find that it is helping you, do not credit the change entirely to the climate, but rather to the different surroundings and coloring, which have more to do with the cure than has the change of climate. If you cannot affort a vacation, change the colorings of your home and dress, and you will find that this proves just as effective.

In color therapy the use of the red ray seems to promote healing, but sores exposed to this ray will invariably develop inflammation and pus, which may be very quickly healed by an exposure to the blue and the green light. Coagulations of the blood will not be as good under the red ray as it is under the blue. Honey gathered from all red flowers, red clover, for example, has a much stronger and sweeter taste than that collected from other flowers.

If red were reduced to the value of pink or rose, its vibratory effects would be reduced accordingly. Therefore, when speaking of red, we use that term implying the greatest depth of color.

During the days of prohibition, when many private citizens were given to the fascinating pastime of making home brew, they discovered that covering the ingredients with a red cloth hastened the fermentation. The rising of bread dough is also hastened by the influence of the red ray. An experiment was made with eggs that were found to be fertile. These were placed under the red ray, but they did not hatch.

In experimenting with people of varying skin pigmentation, it was found that the darker the skin the less the person was affected by the red ray. One would naturally conclude, therefore, that red is not a color for light-complexioned people but rather a color for the darker skinned people and the brunette.

Tests were made of dark-skinned natives of South America, and it was found that red lacked the effect of producing the signs of nervousness, but rather produced mirth and good cheer.

Babies of this generation have the good fortune of being more peaceful and happy than those born in the days of our grandparents. It was customary for women in the earlier days to wear red flannel bandages around the body during gestation. One can safely say that some of the influence on the temperament of the newly born child was evidenced by its reaction and its crying spells.

Don't make the mistake of feeling that if you have been particularly fond of red, it would not be wise to use it as you have been in the habit of doing. This is a mistaken conception since each of us has a favorite color or preference for certain color combinations. It is right that we should have these preferences, since it helps to make life more interesting.

No one need feel irritated when under the influence of any color or color combination, even if it is not his favorite hue, if the color combinations are kept in even balance according to their speed vibrations. It is really only when a color is out of balance that it jars the nerves of one who is susceptible to the effect of color variations.

A dark person might surround himself with more red than a light-skinned individual, who would scream and rebel when subjected to the red ray. However, one can use all the red one wants to if, in some way, it is balanced with other speeds that could be tamed down to a common acceptable level. Red should not be despised. It is beneficial and wholesome and must not be discarded. It should be used as one would a condiment or dressing, not as a basic food.

In short, red in its entirety should not be used to surround the growing child, but is good if used in moderation. Toy manufacturers should heed this.

The color, red, has little place in the nursery scheme of directions. Yet toy manufacturers use red because it is more attractive and holds the attention of the child to the greatest degree. It is interesting that the small child feels the attraction of red more than any other color. Try placing a green object of the same shape as the red one before the baby and he will reach out first for the red.

When a person is corpulent he should not use much red, since tones of cooler colors will make better surroundings, and the individual will feel more at ease if the cooler colors dominate.

If you want your child to sit still and be quiet, do not dress him or her in red. If you, yourself, are nervous and excitable when dressed in red, discontinue wearing it for a period. After you have done this for a while, you will notice that you can again wear it with good results.

Chapter III

PERSONALITY AND CHARACTER ANALYSIS
THROUGH COLOR

What type are you? Are you feminine, conservative, whole-some, executive, or dramatic? Are you the red, orange, yellow, green or blue personality type? What type is your husband? Do your colors and his blend? Every human being has a color that is individual to him, a color that is compatible with his nature, that pleases him, and is most gratifying to his emotions. By their colors you can know them! As soon as you make a color choice, the following general facts are likely to be true:

In your dress, if you are the feminine type, soft pastels are good alone or as accents to dark colors. If you are the conservative type, clear cool colors, with white as contrast, are good. If you are the wholesome type, warm colors and soft pastels with navy blue and not much black are indicated; whereas the executive type wears black and other dark shades. The dramatic type often wears black with strong accents; pastels only in neck wear and sharp contrasts, when using two-color combinations.

Faber Birren noted color engineer has invented this system of color character analysis to type. The information gathered above is his discovery and findings, gathered from "Character Analysis Through Color."

Color serves an entertaining method of revealing innate per-sonality traits. The person being analysed takes active instead of passive participation by expressing his likes for certain colors.

"If you love red, you are an extrovert and struggle ardently

12

to overcome your natural timidity. Others of your hue are Cellini, Villon, Lord Byron, Lincoln and Theodore Roosevelt. You are vigorous, impulsive, courageous and given to action. Deep sympathy lies within you, and you could bleed for humanity. Life means a lot to you; you want to *live!* You want your existence packed with thrilling events! Red puts you at the mercy of life, and people at the mercy of life either miss it or surmount it. You had better marry someone of your own hue, or someone orange. You could get along with a green personality, but a blue one would be liable to heckle you."

"If you choose orange, you are a person to be envied. Amongst your type was F. D. Roosevelt, Falstaff, P. T. Barnum and Mark Twain. You are the "Hail Fellow Well Met" type! You *ought* to have a grand love of life! You have enviable taste in food, and make a true gourmet. You like to make special cakes and special cocktails so that all your friends will rave! In your eagerness to attract others to your side, and to be attractive, and to please, you are likely to neglect the spiritual values of life. You are as social as can be! At ease with saints and sinners! You have great fluidity of speech, a big smile and an engaging laugh! You want to make people cherish you, for you hate to be alone. Live true to your type! Don't bother if people say you lack profundity! You have what so many others lack—eloquence. Your sense of humor could be perfected through more training; it is naturally quick anyhow. The world likes people of your hue! You make an ideal bachelor, but you could marry one of your own color and go merrily through life! For relaxation to mind and soul, a blue type would be best of all for you."

"Pick yellow, and you are intellectual, an idealist, fit company for Buddha, Confucius, Spinoza and Kant. Extremely pure in type, you have a high mind, but not that of a dreamer. You have grand ideas, meticulously shaped, and perfectly designed to do for the world and for people. You long for the profound admiration of others, you are a mental lone wolf; you are a safe friend and a reliable confidant. You are exacting of others, and a born Evangelist. As a philosopher you love others. You could marry almost any color type and be content. Your own hue, and purple, are best, however."

"If you love green, which is nature's color, you will be in company with Shakespeare, Anatole France, and Will Rogers. Green gives you a universal viewpoint—the ability to understand the problems of others, to be tolerant and liberal. Yours is a good mind, smooth and amiable. Because your mind is clear and without prejudices, you have trouble seeking out the permanent values in life. It is so easy for you to fall in love. Your fancies will be attracted to many rather than a few. You want money. You are courageous but never reckless. There is a little of everything for you. Guard your better qualities. Don't neglect the natural beauty of your mind. Try to be understanding rather than merely educated. A good brain is one that *thinks*, and not only "knows all the answers." Your name might not get into the encyclopedia, but people will love you once they know you. Green personalities make good husbands and wives, because they get along with any mate. Red would be your best choice; the courage you lack might lead you merrily into the world which you adore."

"Blue is the choice of the introvert and the natural born conservative. Most Republicans are blue, as were Coolidge, Washington, Franklin and Lindberg. If you pick blue, you might have Nordic blood in your veins. You are sensitive to others, and you have a secure hold on your enthusiasms. You have weight to your character, even though it might be a trifle cumbrous to others. When you sin your conscience bothers you but you will sin just the same. You are a good student, and said to have sound judgment and a deep sense of responsibility. Don't confuse mole hills with mountains. You are cautious in dress, word and action. You lead a sober life. You are a born executive. What troubles you most is your inability to let go. Stupidity annoys you as much as superior intelligence. You make a perfect bosom friend, and a safe mate is found in your own color type or in green. However, if a male you are likely to choose a red or orange maiden, because your dormant emotions crave stimulation. Then after marriage you are likely to want to change this charming red or orange girl, and ruin everything, for you should not try to change her personality traits."

"If you love purple your characteristics are unusual and exclusive. Choose pure purple and you are a mystery to yourself as well as to others. You will keep company with Voltaire, Pasteur, Jefferson and Poe. Artistic people favor this color, and deserve it inasmuch as their minds are in general of uncommon stamp. They are usually quite satisfied with themselves. Purple lovers are generally blessed by a true sense of values. Here genius is often found, but genius that never promotes itself. One of their greatest charms lies in the subline quality of their minds: an abiding wisdom which they never attempt to force on others. They are adjustable, but not impressionable. They will reconcile themselves, where others will merely give in. They are easy to live with. They don't bother their mates by being too impulsive like the red personalities, nor are they too straightlaced like the blue ones. If you know them intimately they will hide little from you. Yellow makes an ideal mate for purple, however, almost any type will do. There is something divine in this hue, something to be cultivated and explored."

"If you choose brown you are substantial, dependable and steady. You keep company with Rabelais, Dickens, Darrow, You are conservative by nature, rather than by taste. You don't like impulsiveness or show. There is always a sameness about you, a sort of ageless quality that makes people say you never change. You never have to shirk responsibility. People could lend you money and not have to worry. As an epicure, you like good, plain food. You buy things on the basis of quality, but not class—never any excesses for you. You are greatly flattered when people admire your qualities. People call you wise more through the way you act than through what you know. You think that conservatism is humanity's chosen virtue. You are the rock of Gibraltar that cannot be budged. Cultivate your mind and try to stimulate it a bit. You make an ideal partner for one who would appreciate you. The orange and green personality type would suit you best."

Color is the universal, international language around us. Every time nature speaks to us it speaks in colors. Our eyes see only 20% of what is going on; 80% is used to recharge the nervous system. That is why many hues, shades and tints are found on the trees so that you can draw that which you need. Long ago a Scotchman discovered a measuring rod for color. He found that at different times of the day, at sunrise, noon, sunset, and midnight, the colors of the universe change. He felt that nature breaks down color into four spectrums. These are nature's divisions and every plant and tree that blooms and lives is confined to one of the four groups. Thus a geranium is in the first group, also a Renoir painting. How do you recognize this yardstick? Well, if a Renoir painting with its colors were transposed to a Van Gogh, it would not be a pretty picture. So each person fits into one of the categories. In brief the explanation of the categories is: sunrise colors, or the Quanta 1. Quanta I is radiant, fresh and warm. They are the strong blues and scarlets (Royal Blues). Every tone enhances every other tone. The second of the Quanta Theory, or Quanta II, belongs to the noon colors, which are vibrant, sharp and dry. Not like

Quanta I colors, which enhance the neighboring color by comparison, these colors equalize on the principle of taking from the strong to add to the weak. Thus you put the stronger colors next to the weak ones and their differences are equalized. Quanta III, or the sunset colors, are irridescent, delicate and chalky. Intensification is the objective. Here the quality of the colors are hard, cold, and thin. Each color sparkles in its intensity beside its neighbor. The Quanta IV, or moonlight colors, blend and merge. They arrive at opalescent effects of glow and luminosity against the weight of rich backgrounds. You, as a person, fall into one of the Quanta colors, and the fruits and vegetables, paintings and surroundings for that type all hold good for you. If you would derive 100% pulling power, take cognizance of the four color families, let them serve you as a yardstick in choosing background and accessories.

If you are the fair blonde, you resemble the white rose whose petals are delicate rose; with clear soft blue eyes, your hair is flaxen or light gold. You might be called the cool blonde. There is also the fair blonde with brown hair. She has the same delicate rose-tinted skin, and pink cheek tones; her eyes may be a clear gray, or blue-gray, or blue. Her hair is soft golden brown.

The rule for women of the fair blonde type, with the absence of any pronounced color of skin, should be to emphasize the complexion with rose colors and those hues that have warmth. If the eyes lack fire or brilliancy then contrasts should be used to enliven them. Green is excellent as it makes the delicate skin color richer. It also increases the power of the eyes by simultaneous and positive reflection, and gives the hair a greater richness and warmth. Remember, choose the divine tones of green, such as olive, sage and moss. The dark greens bleach fair complexions, and that is the last thing the fair complexion requires. Three tints must be preserved or improved in the case of the fair blonde. The white rose petal skin must be warmed, the clear soft blue eyes must be deepened and the hair must be enriched so that it compares in a most effective way with the pale tint of the brow and the color of the eyes. With colors such as red, orange and gold, take care how you use them. Quiet greens are to be preferred. A green hat when there is not green in the dress can have rose colored trimmings combined with white. Orange might replace the rose as well as gold in hat trimmings, but should not be in juxtaposition to the skin. If the eyes are blue, a little orange is effective. Blue is most becoming. It imparts delicate orange tint, which combines with the natural pink and white of the skin. Blue, like green, must be kept light and not positive. A blue dress alone might be ineffective, but blue with white or cream may be freely used to give dress brightness. Avoid the green, red or purple scale. The neutral colors best adapted are slate gray, fawn and drab. Black is good for those with pink in the skin. To relieve it, use light blue, gold, yellow, cerise and red. Watch your fabrics. Choose dead black fabrics, such as velvets. White heightens and sets off the normal pink color of the complexion. Remember that only the palest green can be used in contrast with white. Prefer dead whites without a gloss to any glazed fabric which is trying to the complexion. For golden blondes apply all colors a little deeper. The auburn or ruddy blonde can use the same colors as recommended for the fair blondes but must be deepened in tone so that the blues and greens which add orange or red to the complexion are avoided.

Titian the painter has immortalized the auburn blondes. It is the business of color to tone down the high local blush of the auburn blonde, and to refine and moderate the natural complexion tints. Green is one of the most becoming colors. Delicate greens are preferable to dark greens. The nearer the complexion is to the true auburn blonde type the duller the green should be. Remember the paler the complexion the more normal or positive the green. The more rosy the complexion the cooler the green.

Blue is also a becoming color for the auburn blonde. It follows the same law laid down for green. The deeper the tone of blue the more colored must be the complexion, and the blues which incline toward the green and the gray scales are ordinarily to be preferred to those inclined towards the ultramarine blue. Bright blues of any hue should not be brought in direct contact with the skin. They should be separated from it with semi-transparent material or trimming of white or light gray.

There is in the category of women's beauty the florid brunette with her rich toned skin, inclined towards the golden brown, in some cases leaning to olive, in others to a warm copper complexion. This is the most perfect and commanding of all female beauty. Her eyes are of the darkest and most intense brown—almost black—and she has jet or blue-black hair. She is equivalent to the auburn blonde type. Yellow and red hues predominate. The object of every girl and woman of this type should be to avoid weakening the natural color advantage by using objectionable colors in dress. Colors most becoming to the florid brunette are rich maize color, yellow, and deep gold. They neutralize in a marked degree any surplus yellow which the skin itself may naturally contain. Orange is also becoming. It is to be used for trimmings. Reds may be used effectively. Dark red is to be commended for general dress when associated with brunette complexions naturally rich in red. They neutralize the color of the skin. They also reduce its force at times by simultaneous contrast. Maroon, quiet in its effect, rose pinks, dark blue, olive green are becoming to the florid brunette type. All florid brunettes should avoid light blues, light greens, pale violets, violet pinks and **purples of every** kind. Black imparts fairness to the brunette, and so does white. Always choose a cream white. Relieve the black by glossy or colored trimmings. Velvet is preferable to any other material.

The pale brunette combines a pale skin, tending to the sallow, with deep brown or black eyes and hair of a rich dark brown color. Pale brunette is very beautiful and expressive in type. Powerful contrasts exist between the tone of the skin and the dark shades of eyes and hair. Hence colors harmonizing are best suited for her costumes. That is to say, either light or dark colors will suit her type better than medium ones. Colors of medium intensity between the tone of the skin and the hair hurt the pale brunette. They have a pronounced tendency to reduce the vivid impression which is her greatest charm. It may be said that the pale brunette offers greater color difficulties with regard to her dress than any type of feminine beauty. She is the hardest to dress effectively. Black is a very trying color for the pale brunette. All glossy blacks should be avoided, but black velvet with cream colored trimmings, lace preferred, may be safely adopted as a rule by the pale brunette. Blue must be avoided as it has a positive tendency to lend the complexion an orange hue. A warm brown harmonizes with the complexion, but olive and gray brown should be avoided. Brown has a subdued and quieting effect and is suitable for young girls, and can be used in two or three tones in the same scale of brown. Warm colors are becoming to the pale brunette, but all positive hues must be very cautiously approached. Deep russet, claret, crimson, old rose and broken reds are not likely to affect the palid brunette complexion unfavorably. Gold and maize yellow are good since they form an agreeable contrast to her eyes and hair. The pale brunette must avoid light blues, light or bright greens, violets, purples and pinks. For those who have blue eyes and black hair, with the complexion of the florid or fair brunette, use the same contrast power. Golden hues are especially becoming to this type.

"All the world is a stage" and men and women are the players. You are the leading lady on your own stage. You can dramatize your life and make your existence a masterpiece or a failure. Color is a key to the lock of the invisible forces around us, and its knowledge and understanding will make you seek more beauty and charm and be admired by others. It is everyone's right to aspire to as much beauty and charm as she can attain. You can possess that beauty for your very own for it is imbedded in you. You must only bring it out. It can give you personality, unrestricted and unlimited.

Chapter IV

CHOOSE YOUR RIGHT COLOR

The scarlet flames with passion,
The crimson rays with lust,
The green-blue glows with reason
While murky blue distrust.
The violet-blue for healing,
The cerise of soul spells might.
Orange-yellow is soothing,
While all the colors spell white.
Now white is the symbol of purity and age,
Precious reward for saint and sage;
The inner light in hours of rest,
Color insignia, the best!

As a person delves into the traditions of color, he will quickly realize that throughout the ages human beings have assigned almost the same meanings to various hues of the spectrum. Reactions, in other words, have been nearly the same and have left records of their consciousness to be revealed again today in the hues which we moderns prefer. Because there is color everywhere, the art of choosing the right color can prove to be a great aid to beauty. Thus a woman can brighten her personality amazingly by wearing the right colors.

"Wear your personality on your back," was the advice given to a noted actress by her producer. If women only realized that their exteriors were their visiting cards, they would heed the advice of this producer. The best advice is to discover your own springboard. Colors can mold and give shape to forms that otherwise are meaningless. When man has realized this and takes a hint from nature, he will bring into the world of fashion new colors that are evident every season just as they are evident in the nature world.

Have you ever had a dress in which you looked simply heavenly? Remember how you regarded this gown with awe, and charged it with supernatural power? Have you ever stopped to analyze what it was about this gown that brought out your best personality?

People are born to their own colors—their own rainbow. Thus we have our personal flag, consciously or unconsciously. Just as the gods of the ancients were likened to the sun which emitted rays of light—so does color issue from the human body in the form of an aura. In Persia the aura was studied and its color accepted as a mark of spiritual and mental development. Today, we are not conscious of this influence, yet we exert it continuously.

Each person has three colors that influence him; three colors to keep around him in his personal surroundings and environment: his personal color; his business or expressional color; and his social color. One minute with these colors does more to recharge a person than hours spent in neutral surroundings. It is therefore advisable to have a pillow made of the color that is your personal hue. Since all human beings do something with themselves during the course of their lives, it is necessary for them to become more conscious of their business or expressional colors. Heritage is important but the vital power of our personalities that shines through our expression gives us certain characteristics that are individual to us, which makes it important for us to radiate our true expressional colors.

In order to do that, it is advisable to have the desk blotter and personal stationery, as well as the ink, correspond to your expressional color. This acts as a link. Why not have your surroundings and your clothes also in harmony with your expressional hue? This holds true for your social color as well. In mingling with society it is nice to hold in mind your social color. Thus your clothes should carry out your color tendencies, which makes shopping much easier, since you know immediately the colors you wish to choose. If it is for the business world, you choose your business color. If it is for the social world, you choose your social color.

Did you ever know that you could glamorize your skin tone by the use of colors? For instance, if your skin is white, you may use any color, including black. If you have a creamy skin try wearing canary-yellow, chartreuse-green and golden brown; whereas if you have a pearly skin, your color should be dusty pink, dubonnet, rose and black. For those who have an olive complexion, red, flame, green and brown are good. The rose-tinted damsel should wear rose, peach and green. Now the deep olive-complexioned women should turn to the terra cotta, scarlet, orange and brown.

It is not enough for you to flatter just the skin tones, but it is also necessary to play up to the eyes. So if your eyes are gray your colors should be dusky rose, heather, mauve and chartreuse-green. If your eyes are blue, your color should be powder blue, sapphire, periwinkle, orchid and rose. The hazel-eyed individual finds green, golden brown, coral, tea-rose and peach most becoming. Whereas brown-eyed people lean to brown, green, scarlet, dubonnet, amber and rose-beige. Green-eyed people can wear almost all shades of green, turquoise, aqua and copper. Black-eyed individuals should lean to black, yellow, jade, gold and orange.

There are certain colors that seem to highlight the hair and bring out hidden lights. For example, the ash-blonde may use grays, green, dusky-pink, mauve and heather to achieve this effect. Golden blondes will find their hair highlighted by wearing white, golden yellow, amber, leaf-green, blue and black.

The flaming red-head might accentuate her hair by wearing terra-cotta, chartreuse, tea-rose, golden brown, turquoise and black. The woman with the auburn hair might wear ivory, yellow, green, powder blue, peacock blue, wine, and black. These colors all bring out the hidden glow in women's tresses. Of course the woman with dark brown hair may wear scarlet, emerald, rose-beige, henna, orange and beaver brown to very great advantage. The black-haired individual can accentuate her hair by wearing yellow, beige, chinese red and gold. The gray-haired lady can highlight her hair becomingly by the use of gray, red, old rose, mauve, blue, black and gray. Those with white hair find it very advantageous to use black and white, sapphire, ice-blue, aqua, coral and violet. The colors mentioned can contribute marvelously to the appearance of the person wearing them. Remember always that light colors and glossy-surfaced materials make the individual look larger. Stout people look stouter when they wear weighty fabrics such as tweeds and velvets.

I believe that Guerrin was right when he said that the only thing that mattered was the reaction of colors and what they said to you. Therefore, the next time you look at colors let your imagination wander. When I see a certain shade of purple combined with gold it brings to me the picture of a white peacock, with oh, so faint and yet far away, its wild cry: or, "Don't you remember that little hat?" said sky-blue to me one day, when I saw it placed against a bit of black velvet. The blue immediately evoked a picture in my mind, and I saw the old-fashioned bachelor-button that stood outside the window. The blue was oh, so blue, just like the water in the pond.

Letting Your Imagination wander into the land of color is a wonderful experience. It is only then that one catches the realization that living is an art, and that one of the techniques to interpret life is the language of color, which is really the language

of the emotions or the international language spoken around us
daily. Why not think of flowers as the smiles of angels? They
are really the angelic thought-forms of God, expressed through
His floral agencies on the earth.

Let us play a game, you and I. Let us take an object and
see what it brings to your mind. Take for instance a yellow
daffodil. Yellow always seems argumentative to me, it seems
to have a mind of its own. I should imagine if yellow could
talk our language, we would probably hear about some mili-
tant suffragette. And yet yellow always reminds me of the
story of a woman gently born, who with soft auburn hair, and
great gray-blue eyes, had a smile that looked like abundance.
This woman went to live amongst the poor, and gave shelter
to the needy all day long and sometimes late at night. This
beautiful lady was kept busy binding up aching wounds. The
floor and the walls in her little apartment of mercy were painted
daffodil yellow with vases filled with these flowers standing on
white tables. When asked why she used so much yellow, she
answered, "It is the color of the sun, and these poor people
need the sun so badly, both in their homes and in their hearts,
that I have tried to create a haven of sunshine for them. Many
of them say that they feel better the minute they step inside of
my door. Some of them think that it is some kind of a spell that
I cast, or that I have medicated the air, but it is all yellow that
does it. Yellow, the color of the sun!"

If I were to go on in my imaginings in the land of color, I
would animate apple-green, and ask it what it tells the world.
Immediately in my mind's eye would come the picture of a
girl who was beautiful in both body and soul. She would wear
clear apple-green. Her love for her sweetheart was not allowed
to live long, because she died. I remember seeing her dressed in
the gown of pale apple-green, signifying youth, hope, gentle
love and charity, and it has imprinted itself on my mind since.

Let us see what purple has to say. It always seems to be bragging about velvet and diamonds, kings and courts. The royal purple! It was considered royal because it was a dye that had to be brought from distant foreign lands. This cost so much money that only those that were rich could afford it. Therefore because of its rarity it became known as royal purple.

If we were to talk to pink, apricot, brown and olive, and if we were to listen hard enough, we would be astonished what chatterers these colors are.

People's characters are in tune with certain colors, just as flowers are. This radiant language acts as color-signs. Flowers use this language. Flowers evoke with their fragrance our beautiful thoughts, and like color-tones, tints and music, they draw out the best in our souls, and bring us just a little closer in our feeling to the universal Creator.

Flowers are really the true teachers of art, beauty and refinement, since they inspire our love natures, and increase our vision for terrestial as well as celestial beauty. What lesson is comparable to the lesson of the flowers? "Yet, Solomon, in all his glory, was not arrayed as one of these." The language of color and beauty inspires us and leads us to think God's thoughts, and radiates its fragrance to God's children.

Chapter V

THE SECRET OF POWER THROUGH COLOR

With what variety of boundless form and color is the earth garnished! How does the same air and moisture combine to form so endless a maze of diversity? From the lofty redwoods of the Sierras to the fragrant desert flower in its quiet retreat, the appropriateness and adaptability of each class, color-shade and kind constitutes a million miracles. The greatest Masters, poets, artists, occultists, mystics and spiritualists love flowers. The orientals, as well as Christ, not only loved flowers, but used them as representatives and examples of service, symbols of beauty, art and love.

Ernest J. Stevens was a personal friend of Luther Burbank, the man who not only gathered the human flowers, but talked and communed through flowers with God; not, as he felt, the misunderstood orthodox God of heaven and hell, but the Deity of plants, fruits, color and beauty. Ernest J. Stevens, though dead, lives fresh in my memory and in my flower thoughts, and radiates in spirit the realm of inspiration. We spent many delightful hours together in comparing the flowers and fragrance of the wholesome fruits with their corresponding colors; exchanging our views and research experience on science, health, nature and art.

Professor Ernest J. Stevens was an intellectual soul. He had ingenious strength and extraordinary powers. He believed in his readers and that greatness was within the reach of all of them. He honored them by thinking that they could accomplish much, and they gleaned from his works the inspiration to open up new vistas of thoughts for themselves. Ramona Crosby said of him, "Oh my God, I thank thee, for the gleam of light in this man who carries a torch of light and freedom for the soul; this flame of God that lights the way; this torch of Divinity that heals and blesses us." These lines were dedicated to Dr. Stevens in recognition of his untiring efforts in the cause of humanity.

Miss Beatrice Irwin, lighting expert, has proved through her work that color has a practical bearing on home and personal relationships. She has proved her theory by the installation of a filter system of illumination in homes, hospitals and offices, as well as in places of recreation such as the Strand Theatre in New York. She demonstrated to congresses of illuminating engineers in Washington, Philadelphia, Buffalo and New York. In the following table, I show twelve colors. There is a table for their signs, uses and effects, as well as the properties that the color possesses. The condition for which the color is applied is also included. (*see chart next page.*)

Colors – Hues	Symbols	Effects	Used to Remedy
Red	Danger sign Fire, Blood, War Feverishness	Stimulant (strong)	Anaemia Jaundice Yellow condition of skin
Pink	Friendship Physical love	Stimulant (mild)	Anaemia The blues
Scarlet	Danger Anger Sensuous sex	Stimulant (animal)	Senility Low animal rating
Orange	Wholesomeness	Tonic and Laxative	Low vitality Low tone
Yellow	Relaxation	Nervine Laxative	Nerves Inflammation
Lemon	Pride	Antiseptic Tonic	Exhaustion
Green	Jealousy	Antiseptic Astringent	Poisons Broken bones Malnutrition
Magenta	Sex nature	Sex or creative passion	Heart affections Low blood pressure
Cerise	Creative Psychic	Sentiment or Emotions	Course vibrations
Purple (dark)	Royalty Pride	Emotional Depression subduer	High blood pressure
Blue	Devotion Loyalty Truth	Sedative Healing	Burns Skin diseases
Indigo	Benevolence Coolness Calmness	Narcotic Soothing	Boils Swellings
Violet	Spirituality Sublimity Angelic Love	Germicide Purifying	Fevers Congestions Eruptions Low rating

Chapter VI

COLOR IN ARCHITECTURE

Why do business men and women develop "city nerves?" Why, as the afternoon wanes, do office workers develop office blues? I blame both on the fact that business sections of cities are mostly gray instead of having "lifting" colors of nature around them. Not until man realizes his powers and his vibrations can he fulfill himself.

In ancient Byzantine architecture the most exotic colors were used. They even mixed stripes and checkered effects on the exteriors of their homes. Did you know that it was the Anglo-Saxon, living in northern climates, who was the first to become shy of colors? It was he who began to eliminate them from his surroundings. If Americans were anywhere nearly as conscious about brightly colored buildings as they are about clothes in prismatic shades, then we should find colored office buildings for blond stenographers and tired business men.

It's the lack of color in our architecture that produces that tired feeling. The ideal goal is that cities become more colorful. Then life would be more interesting and cheerful also.

I believe that buildings should suit the needs and general atmosphere of the locality. Green, for instance, should be used as a soothing antidote to relieve the high tension of business in industrial districts. Conversely, suburban regions of peace and quiet should run to red, yellow and orange in order to counteract a too constant calm. Tropical cities have, long ago, used brilliant pinks and blues in their make-up. Even Los Angeles boasts of brightly colored buildings. These would seem rather

31

startling if they were set in the gray, tan and buff coloring of northern and eastern cities.

What could be more suitable than brown paint for Mr. Brown's house, and white paint for Mr. White's house? Why not have houses in colors that harmonize with the dispositions and temperaments of the occupants? Pastel shades for buildings suggest any number of practical uses.

We have made much progress. Color, today, is practically the accepted thing in theatres, signs, decorations and clothing, as well as in all style merchandizing. Of late, however, color has been assailing the consumer market from a new side. Suddenly the kitchen has turned into a colorful panorama.

Everything from gas ranges to salt cellars is being offered in vivid greens, blues and yellows. The bathroom offers us azure curtains and delicately tinted bath-tubs with towel-racks and cushions to match. You might wonder what color is accomplishing for the sale of these products. It is attracting customers, unconsciously, since there is a definite language and meaning for color. Until such time arrives that we learn to interpret this universal color language, will we be at odds with the world. What we need is color training.

It is wonderful to what perfection the eye can be educated. Herschel thought that the skilled workers on the mosaics of the Vatican developed the color sensitivity of the artists to such an extent that they could distinguish hundreds of different shades of color. It is surprising to what perfection the senses can be trained. Weber said that musicians can distinguish notes separated on the scale of sound by only one sixtieth part of musical tone. To what perfection, then, may not the consciousness be raised?

The bridegroom who precipitates the first quarrel at the breakfast table may have been led into it by too much red in the wallpaper. This gives him mental, and often physical indigestion. William Downie, master painter and decorator, said, "Every color rouses some response, either agreeable or otherwise. Loss of appetite, for instance, may simply be due to the decorative scheme of the dining-room. Restlessness might be caused by a jarring note in the living-room. Subconsciously, we do react to colors and that reaction is even more important than we realize."

There are many inherent and latent potencies of nature which await to serve man as soon as he has mastered himself enough to be trusted with their use. Color has always been a power as strong as electricity, but we have been ignorant of its laws so that instead of governing it, it has ruled us. Remember, we in the manifest world are never exempt from color influence. It is an appealing messenger, attracting attention by its beauty and variableness. Chromalingua, or color language, is really a universal crochet needle that would join people together all over the world by teaching them the inner meanings of nature. It is the medium used by Nature as well as by man to convey instantaneous impressions to the mind. It is really the most accurate and exact medium, and has also the added function of expressing prophecy.

God's word is most perfectly recorded in the heart of man. Color is, however, the most accurate symbol of interpretation of the word, "God." It is really not necessary for you to learn to read in order to live, but it is necessary for you to know *how* to read in order to live life more fully. It is therefore very wise for you to read the color language so that you might translate nature and the story of life in all its natural manifestations that you may live more harmoniously with Nature and the finer forces. Why not accept the fullest enjoyment from life? You can only do this by fully understanding the language of color. Everything you see and everything you touch has an element of color in it. You cannot escape this. Therefore it is wise to know more about it. Color is used as the distinguishing factor. It enables us to separate, in our vision, one object from another.

Color has been used by man primarily to express his emotions rather than his thoughts. It is interesting to note that color can be used either constructively or destructively in angelic or devilish service, as a quickener of inspiration or of lust. As chroma-lingua is the language which we cannot but choose to speak, it behooves us to speak it as correctly and beautifully as possible. Believe it or not, there are many educated people who commit glaring errors in the expression of color. They don't know the laws which govern various combinations nor do they realize that these laws are as necessary as the laws that govern associations of words. These same people would consider it a terrible breech to confuse their grammar, but they go serenely on in their ignorance of color language and offend those whose color sense is developed.

The expression of color ideas constitutes a most peculiar art. It cannot be acquired in any degree of perfection except by long and continued practice. Anyone can get the fundamental principles underlying color expression. This enables him to analyze and unlock color schemes for himself. Color gives wings to the flight of imagination, and then the imagination rises on its wings to meet the new presentation.

It is unscientific to doubt the emotional effect of color because we do not understand it properly or deny that a color impression may create a physical as well as mental reaction.

The nature of this mental reaction depends primarily on the understanding of the individual's consciousness or of his individual character. Everyone reacts differently to color sensations since each is a law to himself. Color experiences are so subtle and so intricate that it is only due to the knowledge of their fundamental principles that we are able to interpret their reactions and correlate them with the reactions in our lives.

Color both prompts and stimulates the imagination, and a lack of appreciation of color is often a sign of lack of discriminaton and sensitiveness. People that are color blind often have moronic faculties. The more evolved the individual, the more their color sensitivities are developed. By that I don't mean that all people who are color blind are morons. I simply wish to indicate that there is a blind spot in their spiritual development that needs awakening.

Chapter VII

THE MISSION OF MUSIC & COLOR

I shall not attempt to write a discursive study of the lives of the great composers, or attempt to summarize their influence as exerted on contemporary thought and conduct. A few years ago I made a series of pictures called "Symphonic Films," putting music and color on the screen and showing the character of the music of various composers and the colors it invoked. For instance, Handel's music was shown to be purple—formal, grand and awe-inspiring, expressing, by its glorification of repetition and imitativeness, the strict conventionalism of the Victorian era. If one translates these qualities from the world of music to that of human conduct, a love of outward ceremony and adherence to convention would be shown. Thus Handel identified himself with the force that helped swing the pendulum from the era of moral laxity to the other extreme. If you will remember, one of the main social characteristics of western Europe was the widespread decline in social morals after the Restoration in England and the reign of Louis XVI in France. Handel found it his mission to revolutionize this state of moral laxity, and swung to the profound laws of convention.

This tendency was so great—the feeling of repression and constraint—that it needed a composer like Bach, almost a musical mathematician, to exert a stronger influence over the mentality of people rather than over their emotions. He demonstrates a wonderful unity of idea, which pervades all of his work, as well as a great spirit of logic and respect for conformity to musical law. He might be considered the father of all modern music since he had a great effect on the mental organism through the adept use of dissonance, thus training the thinker to be more pliant and subtle and giving him a newness of outlook. He induced people to greater responsiveness—to new ideas—thus helping to reduce the rigidity of their prejudices which stood in the way of their spiritual advancement. Bach may be called the liberator, the musician who set our thoughts free. With him we link the intellectual yellow.

Next, we come to Mendelssohn. His music is soft, exquisitely tender, heralding joy and sympathy. Hence, people after listening to his compositions would melt, becoming sympathetic and more tolerant towards their environment and friends. He cheered the weary-hearted by his glowing gaiety, and like Florence Nightingale, went and healed the sick, scattering his musical notes as soothing medicine to those who listened. The predominant color produced by Mendelssohn's music of sympathy is apple-green.

The musician who was destined to arouse compassion, charity and pity by picturing the plight of the unfortunate—was Beethoven. He expresses a vast array of strange emotions, and speaks about the inner feelings of man that ordinarily are not portrayed. He thus promoted sympathy to an extent that was previously unknown. His music strives to bring about a greater unity between the mind and the heart, thus producing understanding. He releases the subconscious and liberates the emotions, ridding them of their repressions. He is the forerunner of the modern psychiatrist. He produced musical psycho-analysis. His colors are the warm shades of red.

Chopin became known as the mirror of the aspirations, thwarted desires and ambitions of the intellegentsia of his day. He tried to make beauty a religion; to preach the gospel, that, "To refrain from doing a thing, if unbeautiful was better than to refrain because it was merely unconventional," as Scott wrote about him. On the whole, Chopin advocated the transmuting

of baser elements and emotions to a higher level of consciousness—to service. This high spirituality indicates the color
blue.

Schumann produced the only music that is capable of teaching development of young people, which has a way of affecting
the subconscious of the adolescent. The spirit of his music especially excites and stimulates the egos of backward children, un-
shackling their childish repressions and, like sunshine on a
flower, encouraging them to develop their potentialities. His
is the golden color of sunshine. Sir Walter Scott puts this very
aptly in those of his writings which deal with Schumann.

When one speaks of Wagner, one is inclined to think of the
exotic and neurotic side of this composer's nature, but Wagner
was transcendent also in his conception of the standards of
composition. His music transmutes the lower emotions to the
very highest levels of idealistic service. His keynote is unity
in diversity. Scott says, "Socialistically speaking, Wagner's
music was the prototype of the principle of cooperation." Wagner's ideals of unity, his romantic, heroic efforts, have served
to engender a spirit of intense national cohesion, the basic principles having been harnessed to a lesser purpose than the broad
idea of world unity.

In a more spiritual sense his music symbolizes the return
of the prodigal son or the principle of regeneration. It shows
that each individual soul is unified and joined with the all-em-
bracing soul, making a chain of divine octaves, through which
the One spirit flows. It points out in symbolic form that the
Father pervades everything. Wagner was really the first to
show and portray that love is God. Wagner had rare flights to
Buddhic consciousness, which are are not without their effect
on people who are capable of responding to these lofty vibrations and who are then transported and raised in an exalted
plane of selfless love to a state of unity, the ideal brotherhood.

Only those knowing the spiritual value of music, only those who are able to hear *clair-audiently* the music of the spheres, are able to comprehend the subtle blends and perfect harmonies of Wagner. Perhaps the rainbow in its entirety seems most appropriate; however, we can assign to him a purplish-red.

César Franck demonstrates brotherhood principle. His out pouring of love towards his pupils won him the title of Father, and they became so attached to him that they cared for him as their own. César Franck's characteristics are love and seemingly tireless service. He had great reverence in his soul for God. It is said on very good authority that he often would be found kneeling in the corner of the gallery, prostrating himself at the altar before the Almighty Presence. It was thus that César Franck came into communion with the Higher One whose inspiration led him to translate the language of Color Music with great devotional ardor. It was thus that he formed the groundwork for many of his sublime melodies, such as "The Beatitudes." He gave of himself unstintingly. He felt it his mission to dispel disease and sickness in the lives of those he reached, and designed his music to further this end. His works are therefore contemplative, not ecstatic; and those who surrender themselves to his kind of influence recover from the agitations of their souls and find themselves lifted above self-centeredness. César Franck's music pours like a healing balm and harmonizes the subtler bodies, bringing them into alignment and attuning them to nature's finer forces. He can be labeled as the "Musical Missionary." Sir Walter Scott writes about him, "César Franck's inspiration poured down through his subtle bodies, thereby creating an exquisite chord on the higher planes." His color is violet.

Débussy was the interpreter of the nature world. He captures in his illusive harmonies the zephyrs of the trees, the rippling of the brook, the swish of the grass, and the countless melodies of nature. He acts as a bridge between the seen and the unseen. Nature's music is so subtle in its infinite variety, that only through his notes of sublimated melodies are soothing harmonies produced. Sir Walter Scott puts it very aptly, "if birds were actually to sing tunes, they would call on us like the cuckoo, but never the song of the thrush or the blackbird; it always eludes us." Débussy imitates through his music the great forces that work in nature. Just as each animal and bird make its ovation to the rising sun in music of adoration, so does Débussy render adoration to Mother Nature. He shows the mischieveousness of the nature spirits, such as the gnome and the elf, bringing forth the inner side of music in order for us to compare it with the outer. This inner melody is made by the mischievousness of the nature spirits, such as the gnome by butterfly wings, whereas the outer music is more or less portrayed by the sighing of the wind, the rippling of the stream, and other outer manifestations of the nature world. Débussy had the knack of reproducing with remarkable agility this inner music. He was so concerned with presenting the sounds of this earth plane in a very true-to-nature manner that he might easily be dubbed an inventor of a new kind of music. A soft green best describes his work.

Ravel took upon himself an unusual mission and a profound one; he tried hard to reveal the beautiful in the ugliness of nature. We owe him a great debt of gratitude for the change of attitude toward the unseen. Popular magazines began to print articles dealing with fairies, books were published on folklore, and those who were scoffed at as visionaries because their psychic perceptions were developed were taken with more seriousness than had formerly been accorded to them. All this we owe to the influence of Débussy and Ravel. Ravel's color is the rose-pink he cast over the drabness of the outer world.

Scriabin was the first composer to combine metaphysics with symphonic music. He sensed that his mission was to convey a spiritual message, and like Wagner he wanted to produce music that would benefit the human race.

In his greatest work, Mysterium, he expresses spiritual ideas, designed to have an actively spiritualizing effect on his audience. In his other works such as Prometheus, or Poem of Fire, he uses the subtle harmonizing formula of chromatic contradiction in various parts. He thus produces an effect of natures spirits, an unusual quality and an unearthly music, which reaches the souls of those who listen. His color is deep blue.

Chapter VIII

COLOR AND ITS RELATIONSHIP TO THE THOUGHT WORLD

"Thoughts are things and a small drop of ink, falling like dew upon a thought, produces that which makes thousands, perhaps millions, think."

Thoughts *are* things, and that is literally true. There has been an instrument invented in Paris that completely brings this out. It's a camera, by which thoughts can be photographed, producing thought-form pictures. The photographs show varied forms. I have seen it and have been delighted especially when they showed me the thought-form picture of love, which had the form of a butterfly.

I was so inspired by this idea that I made a few drawings, myself, of the thought-forms of the emotions and their relationship to expression and color. I called them auric portraits. Thus I have depicted the various leaders of the world. Instead of making thought-forms, I tried to show the colors emanating from the mental, physical and spiritual bodies of the person I was drawing. This auric painting was to act as a record of the accumulated thought-forms and character of the individual. It was like an invisible bank, showing the reservoir of strength and weakness.

Our greatest salvation in life will be when we are able to illustrate the thoughts of humans. Only then will we master our thought processes visibly.

When we can show "the man who wants proof, from Missouri," photographs and actual pictures of his thoughts, we will be able to convince him. Anger and hatred are ugly thought-forms. When he has been made to understand that perhaps this is what his thinking looks like, he will, through vanity and pride, take an interest in controlled thought. He will become convinced that to master the art of controlling his thought-processes he will be doing his part in establishing the well-being of the world.

Thought, on being radiated from the mental body, is of a fibrous, vaporous appearance. It portrays the various color-tones of its essential character. If we think with positiveness and strength of purpose we dispatch these thoughts, and they carry with them a certain amount of Prana, that which gives them a shining luminous energy with healing power and magnetism. These various wave-lengths of thoughts, emitted by human beings, attract and are attracted by thoughts of a similar nature. Just as clouds assemble into groups and layers in the earth's atmosphere, so the waves of thought form thought-strata in astral space. These thought particles, forming the clouds, are of different rates of vibration, and so the identical space may be charged with thought-matter of innumerable wave-lengths, yet each will be at liberty to intermingle without dissipating each other. There is, of course, no assimilation between thoughts of dissimilar natures, since there is a law of similarity which attracts thoughts only of similar character which are affinities of each other, and amalgamates them for a time.

The human being is like a radio. It is a receiving as well as a broadcasting station. Therefore, the distance to which thought-power can radiate really depends on the essential nature and the resistance which it encounters. For instance, waves in the lower types of astral matter are passed over by those of higher vibration. The higher, positive thought with its strong beneficent tonic and pranic energy has thus a higher potential power. In other words, a man of strong will, with a vigorous positive thought, radiates unconsciously, or if very developed, consciously. He is impregnated with a supply of Prana that is equal to the force of his purpose. Such thoughts, when directed unselfishly, travel unwaveringly, empowered by their own and similar qualities, often reaching their destination instantaneously. They are powerful because they are left practically unopposed on their own vibratory level—like a light dispelling the darkness, or a peal of music breaking the silence. Thus is set into operation a level of mental matter, rarely used, and the radiations caused thereby touch on the mental body of most people at a point where it is outstandingly dormant. This gives to such a thought the peculiarities of the snowball, gathering and developing as it goes along. It tends to elevate, enlighten and universalize a man's thought, no matter in what direction it may be working. It thus produces immeasurable benefits, not only to the thinker but also to those in association with him, since its tendency is to awaken the higher portion of the mental body.

Can you imagine what stupendous result we would have were we to organize this force? The very fact that the results of the thought-power of a single individual have been demonstrated leads one to believe that the thought of a score or more people simultaneously directed toward a worthy purpose will achieve a greater result by unity rather than by their separate thinking.

There are many of the human race that act as practitioners and healers to help their fellow men through thought vibration. Some of us have experienced the effect of these color-radiant thoughts sent our way, but we have no conception of the cause of the changed feeling, which brought with it renewed strength and positive courage.

Thought waves are often, of course, handled unconsciously

by men of selfish desires and aims. In that way there are many
people affected by undesirable thought waves. They need not
fear being affected, however, if they will but learn to develop
a mental aura of love and faith. This consciousness is impervi-
ous to the strongest thought-waves which may be projected
against one, which may be met on the astral plane. The higher
the aura of the thought the stronger its vibration. Thus the
weakest person who realizes this, and affirms the truth of universal love is far more protected and powerful than the individual of a stronger personality, who lowers himself to selfish
ends. The highest radiation of this power is possessed only by
those who have earned it; those of great spiritual development,
who have long since dispensed with the lower aims, ambitions
and desires of the undeveloped man.

Such developed ones are constantly radiating thought-waves
of strength and help, which may be drawn upon by those who
are in need. In other words, they form a bank or reservoir of
strength.

To tune into this universal radiation, one has to elevate one's
consciousness to the heights of this pinnacle and make a conscious mental demand. Immediately, therefore, one attracts to
oneself the strong, helpful waves of spiritual thought which are
emanating from the minds of the teachers and helpers of our
race. Their object is to enrich the ether with positive thought-
waves. It is the building of this reservoir of positive thought
that makes it possible for humanity to pass through the darkness of selfishness and negative thinking and to go forward
through the help of the power of this light.

The only thing that we ought to fear in the world of thought-
forms are the corresponding forms of any base thoughts that
we might harbor. It is advisable, therefore, to clean house
within our own minds first, before we permanently attach to
ourselves low, selfish thought-forms. We are then inviting

thought-forms of similar character, which might be lurking in the psychic atmosphere, and which might attach themselves to our minds and urge us forward to do things that we would otherwise reject doing. Remember that every thought has a color, and therefore, if we do not wish to invite such an unbidden guest, we should well consider the color-key of our emotional thinking. as, like rays of the sun, the emanations go forth into the atmosphere.

Every time we plant a strong desire, we create a thought-form which will work toward the fulfillment of our wishes, no matter what they are, good, or bad. Thus we attract to us and we are drawn toward things by their thought-forms according to the magnetisms of their color vibrations. These thought-forms are enlisted as the most powerful helpers of humanity since they never are too tired to do their work. In other words, if you don't want action at once, then don't send forth strong thought-forms unless they meet with your inner approval or the approval of your higher self. You will, otherwise, become enmeshed in the results or consequences arising from your own projections. Then only will you learn and suffer much, finding that your psychic powers should only be used for higher purposes, and never for degrading ones. It is interesting to note that we are punished by the things themselves, not for them.

Never, never allow yourself to send forth a strong desire thought to injure or degrade another. No matter what the pretext might be there would be but one result and that would be deep suffering for yourself. It acts as a boomerang for the projector. Speeded up by the energy from the impact of a pure mind, it becomes twice as powerful as the original thought-telegram.

I once read a little story, that has implanted itself in my mind, illustrating this fact. In a certain portion of India where the use of fakirs was much depended upon, a prince once visited. He was staying with his brother whom he envied with all his heart. His jealousy grew until one day he found himself visiting a Black Magician. He enlisted the services of this man to annihilate his brother and paid him huge sums of money. One day the other brother, who was a God-fearing man, felt depressed and annoyed, not knowing that he felt the negative vibrations directed against him. The good man was inspired to sit down and pray. Suddenly, he heard a voice say, "Draw a circle around yourself, son." He obeyed, not knowing the meaning of this gesture. Suddenly there appeared before him, just outside the circle in which he had seated himself, a black knight on a black steed. The knight galloped towards him, pointing his spear, but as soon as he touched the circle, he fell off his horse, dead. The horse scampered and whinnied a little and then collapsed too. The brother watched this phenomenon, puzzled but deeply impressed. He did not know that this thought-form, created by the Black Magician, had been directed toward him in order to take his life. His prayer and protective aura had served as an invincible steel armour against this enemy of the light. The Black Magician, however, felt the boomerang of his own thought-form at the moment that the black knight and steed collapsed. The thought-form directed to kill the brother, rebounded on him and killed him instead.

Those who might have studied the radionics of thought know the tremendous possibilities which swing wide open to those who wish to tune in and utilize the stored-up thought-forms which have been energized and issued from the great minds of the thinkers of the past and present. There are always available, as in a universal thought-bank, the thoughts necessary for the demand of the ones who might have use for them. It's really astonishing that so little has been written or presented on this subject.

There are such tremendous creative possibilities for those

who know how to tune into these ideas that it leaves one numb to think of these unlimited opportunities. A man, working along almost any line today, might attract to himself the most inspiring thoughts, related to his particular line of endeavor if he would draw from the thought-bank, which is packed full of his source material.

The greatest inventions, such as the steam-engine, as well as the most beautiful architecture and illumined books have come to some of their originators in this manner, although those in whose minds they settled never quite realized the source of their ideas.

Often a man applies a considerable amount of thought to some subject, then, relaxing, throws open to the outside world his thought influences. He is astonished to feel, rushing into his receptive mind, the ideal plan for his work, invading his field of consciousness from the universal thought-bank, causing his work of art to be born.

Action is the only prayer in life. Unmaterialized and unexpressed thoughts that are sent out with considerable force will seek an outlet, and will be drawn to the attuned mind of anyone who is willing to express it into action. For example, if an ingenious thinker evolves an idea which he, himself, has not the strength to utilize, his thoughts go to a man of sufficient energy to manifest and operate them. Without knowing it, these thought-forms will pour into his mind, and he will feel himself uplifted and inspired. The law really is completely impersonal. It does not care to whom and through whom it works, as long as it realizes itself.

I have noticed that no matter how complicated and intricate a problem is there is a solution for it. The method is a simple one. Put aside your own theories and assume a receptive, tolerant attitude toward all thoughts that might be associated with the subject. Put the matter completely out of your mind.

Then open yourself up to the universal bank of thought, and lo and behold, before you know it, the solution will flash upon you just like a streak of lightening, and you will be surprised at your own contact possibilities.

Few, if any, have appreciated the underlying cause of the law of this thought-world. Even though the world's greatest thinkers, lecturers and writers have experienced examples of it, few of them have been able to review the technique of their efforts so they could reveal it to the world. They have given credit to everything but the universal thought-bank for their ideas. The world is crowded with an abundance of excellent unexpressed ideas. These thoughts are just lying dormant, waiting in readiness for someone to pick them up and express them, and bring them into life's stream. Therefore, it behooves us all to make an extra effort at becoming consciously conscious to develop an awareness of life.

You will then appreciate and understand that there can't be any monopoly or individual ownership of ideas. We are all but temporary receptacles or instruments, according to our own individual capacity for reception. Can't you see how wrong it is, then, for anyone to want to own an idea? There are many private individuals, as well as business concerns, who want to monopolize ideas, restricting others from using or improving them. Remember, we are but temporary receptacles, to be used only as long as we have the capacity for receiving the ideas and letting them pass through us, working them out in the measure of our strength for carrying them on to others. The keynote there again is service and the good of the all. When we realize this for ourselves, we have found the keynote of living. It seems paradoxical that the only way we can own an idea is to give it away, or that the only way we can have an idea is to put it to its most useful service. Thoughts and ideas that we share with others are the only ones that we may retain, and they are forever ours.

Because there is no monopoly of ideas, I must confess that all my ideas, my treasures of thought have been at some time received from diverse sources, whether they be tangible or intangible. They have come to me via people. teachers and books; from physical and super-physical worlds—in fact, from all over. Just like contributary rivulets of a main stream, these ideas and thoughts have come to me, and I am giving them to you, simply acting as a vehicle. I, therefore, do not make any grand claims of originality for my work, since there is but really one source—the universal bank of ideas.

Let all research workers, inventors and earnest students of the Light who draw unknowingly from the universal storehouse of abundant knowledge and thought become conscious of this technique and release the source of their ideas. Anyone that blocks the flow of the exchange of ideas and thoughts, anyone who wants sole ownership or monopoly, is violating the fundamental law of being.

I am so happy in the realization of being a conscious receptor that I wish to give thanks to those whose works and ideas have been planted in the universe so that I might draw on the universal thought-bank. I give to you the fruits of these ideas so that you may put them into active service.

Who are we to say that this universe is not constructed on the principle of a phonograph record? Every thought, every event and every action has a speed of vibration. This vibratory speed is impressed on the ethers, using the same principle of the phonograph record. Just like the needle of the victrola that scratches the groove and simulates the melody or sound on it, so we, through our thinking, act accordingly. We might term ourselves as ether-needles. Isn't it thrilling to think that all the speeches and masterful thoughts of all time can be brought out and into alignment with the present? Just through our contact with them we can draw away the curtain of the past, thus revealing the present and making the present our future. This explains the phrase, "There is no such thing as time in the universe." All time is here with us now in the present. As we work upon it and realize its ideas, we bring ourselves into attunement with the source bank of the universe, which is eternal.

For those who are in need of better health it is wonderful for them to know that the same principle that applies to thoughts applies to health. All the magnetic and healing thoughts exist and circulate in the ethers today. One may draw to himself all of these with the correct color radiance. This will aid him in overcoming the moods of discouragement and depression.

The universal health-bank operates throughout the ethers, sending its currents into the universe. There is tremendous magnetism and force, waiting to be drawn into the individual through his power of will, thought, breath and food.

This is not universally understood. People make frantic gestures to attain health without knowing that their goal is already realized, and the only thing that they have to do is to put themselves into attunement with it. The reservoir of healing energy in the thought-centers of the health-bank can be drawn upon by anyone who needs it in this world.

The first principle of tuning in on the universal health-bank is: free the mind of all prejudice and hide-bound thoughts. The technique is so simple it is really a matter of demanding, and then relaxing in the demand, bringing oneself in tune with a response. When you enter a room and press the button for the electric light, you are not assailed with doubts but you are convinced that there will be light. Apply the same principle in tuning in to the health-bank. It is really too bad that this underlying principle of health is not expressed more often. Even amongst the workers of the field, this knowledge does not seem to be recognized.

There should be a universal understanding that the ethers are crowded with radionic centers or source-reservoirs that can be tapped at will. In most instances the symptom rather than the cause of disease is treated, and the fundamental laws of the universe or the art of being are left hanging in abeyance, undisturbed by both healers and patients.

Chapter IX

COLOR AND ITS INFLUENCE ON OUR FUTURES

You, who read this book, kind friend,
Be lenient to my thoughts expressed,
I cannot tell you half I feel,
Far more within my soul is pressed.

The wonderful gift of color perception has made it possible to touch the emotional side of human organisms. It is through color in nature and through the use of color in painting, in drama, in music and last but not least, in poetry, that we suspect its wonderful possibilities. There are some very highly gifted natural-born colorists with a gift for color harmony. However, to blend the various hues, tints, tones and shades is never an easy process.

Color plays a more important part in the phenomena of the abstract than in the world of the objective or visible. It is in both planes, however, a most exact and accurate registration of vibrations. In fact it is the most exact registration we yet have discovered. Few indeed, can appreciate the greatness and importance of the influence which color has exercised on human affairs.

The old painters and masters had an intuitive perception of color symbolism, which was indicated in the carefully depicted nimbus around the heads of the saints. The same colors were used over and over again in the robes of the holy ones. Saint Agnes, in an article written for a South African magazine, says, "We have paid very dearly for our modern civilization by los-

53

ing during its construction many fine perceptions and enjoyments, one of the most exquisite being transcending color vision."

While the scientific minds of the age give credence to nothing but the five physical senses and their testimony and regard clairvoyance and clairaudience as supernatural phenomena it is nevertheless true that the latter were perfectly understandable to the earlier races.

Humanity lost its power of super-physical functioning only as it became enmeshed in materiality. Its spirit became increasingly enthralled in the bondage of the senses, the greed for gold and the lust for power. Materialism could have no place in the early day of civilization when the sons and daughters of Light walked the earth in all their radiance.

Then none but those of kindly heart and noble thought could occupy a throne. Because his radiant body was visible to the smallest child. Light reigned by right divine, of inherent power and spirituality. Clairsentience was universal and none could assume virtue if he had it not.

The goal for those who tread the ancient path of enlightenment will lead them some day to awaken in a spiritual garden. They will awaken to a state of consciousness that will be so beautiful and sweet that the soul will be bathed in celestial music and in beauty such as there are no words in this language to describe nor any art on this plane of consciousness to depict.

Only in brief moments in our present stage of development can we grasp this as we taste of great beauty and joy or inspiration. Before we can reach such desirable heights, there are a few things that we must change. One of the most difficult things to do is to fill our own life so full of constructive activity that it is impossible for us to find time to mind other people's business.

Before we can even hope to tread this path, we must overcome our love of gossip. It is said by one of the masters that gossip is our most serious offense, and we must become conscious of this fault in order to be used for higher purposes.

I believe that we must till the gardens of our hearts and minds before they can bloom as the flowers of the field, and by their blossoming forth, the earth itself will blossom like a full blown rose. If only we could become devoted to this idea, there is no doubt that with untiring work we would realize our goal. First those who see it and work for it and then the rest of mankind would become a race of divine men and women. The very sighting of this ideal is in itself proof that it exists and might be attained.

If only we could keep our natures open to higher influences, our souls would be like harps touched by master hands, awakened from silence by glorious influences. A person can, by understanding his own mental, physical and spiritual needs, make use of color in his environment. Did you know that every time you set free a vibration on the physical plane, it penetrates to the plane of emotions and physical thoughts? Those who lack sympathy will find that by using the color green they can arouse themselves to feel the thoughts of sympathy. All of us should vow to live the virtues that are suggested by colors. By doing so, there will result a deliberate building of ourselves.

Our goal is to try to teach humanity to make everything about us as beautiful as possible. It is really only through the beauty of form, color, perfume, sound and movement that the Divine can manifest itself in all its richness and fullness.

The expression of divine life is blocked when there is a want of beauty in any of these things. It is only in the deep realization of this fact that we can bestir ourselves to beautify our cities, our halls and our homes. The future spells great changes in our homes and public buildings.

The drab building materials we now use shall be replaced by glass and plastic bricks, which will be so constructed that the rays and waves of the cosmos shall be able to penetrate them and "Bring the outdoors indoors." The box-like type of building which we find etched against our skies shall be replaced with the curved corner and a far stronger system of circular construction. Everything in the universe is based on the circle and only man develops his nest on the principle of the square. If the builders of these houses could have but glimpsed the wondrous beauties of worlds which interpenetrate the one open to our physical eyes (of which nature is really the reflection), the building of row on row of grotesque monstrosities such as our tenements might never have taken place. These tenements are like monumental diseases projected from the lower mental states of self-centered industrialists. They can hardly be considered pleasant memorials of these architects' visits on this planet.

There is not a corner in the nature world that is the ugly equivalent of our tenement houses. Only when there is a universal building plan, based on the cellular system, will the advantages over the old system be realized. Better lighting, color combinations and acoustics will enter hand in hand.

In the new age of lights, tones and colors, public buildings such as churches and concert halls will epitomize all the better principles of living. This also applies to schools. Thus, we will see a greater use of pale green, which stands for sympathy; a greater application of yellow, since it lifts one into inspiration; and more of the color blue, which brings peace and rest to the soul. This is a brand new application of lighting and color principles, since it makes use of the psychological effect of color as well as the physical effect heretofore used. Thus the harmful effect of the yellow and red rays in our electric light bulbs will not be present. Instead, we will bring the day-light to the night, saving our eyes and nerves as well as millions of dollars.

We are on the verge of a new cycle of constructive experience, even though it might appear to us that destruction is rife. Destruction clears the way; it's like cleaning up a room by disordering it first before we tidy it up. Only the clear-sighted can glean the cleaning up process that is taking place through destruction. It is better to have things brought into daylight rather than letting them ferment in dark corners.

Sound will enfold itself in our understanding as we grow to appreciate its creative power both nationally and individually. It is said on good authority that in certain western countries the profound effect of the music of popular composers is receiving increased prominence and is producing an indelible effect on the national mind.

The singer of the future will have a splendid role as he understands that his voice can become a channel for vibrations of lofty thoughts and ideals as well as emotions. It will then be the privilege of the singer to pour fourth spiritual thoughts and feelings that deliberately express his highest ideals. Only when the song is sung in the correct key will the good be materialized. It is from that idea that we glean the power lying dormant within us. Just as there is music of the spheres not heard or sensed by man, so this part of nature will also be unfolded to us.

The future holds a glorious promise. Who are we to say that as we walk along moonlight beaches we will not be able to hear symphonies of music pouring from the pounding waves? As we walk into the mountains we tune into the glorious harmonies of the world-bank of music. These are just speculations on the possibilities that are in store for us, if we will but take the constructive path in life and develop our natures' finer forces.

In the church of the new age the speaker will deliver his sermon to the music of the organ, and the singing of the choir will corespond in key to the text of the lecture. The value of the service will be tremendously increased and impressed on the congregation by this unity. As an example, take the tremendous influence of the village churchbell on its inhabitants. When its notes peal forth they strike the emotional body of the one who hears it. By repeating the sound, the sympathetic chord is aroused in the individual, causing him to feel uplifted and attracted to the church. However, if the emotional note should happen to be different from the one struck by the bell, the response would not be so great. Therefore to avoid any such occurrence the priest of the parish usually plays a complete chime of seven bells. The appeal is then for all, and those who are not aroused by one note might be touched by others. I mention this principle simply because I feel that it will have a far-reaching effect on all departments of our lives in the not too distant future. We shall, I hope, eventually do away with all the harsh, ugly sounds of this present day and age. With the disappearance of these noises, the nation will, on the whole, find a much better sense of well being, and much of our present day neurosis will vanish.

The role of the future composer will offer the possibility of service on a higher plane than we know today. The composer of the future will possess orchestral color-vision. Quoting Sir Henry J. Wood, "Wait for the composer who will possess an orchestral color-vision wider than any known to us today. He will be worthy of his instrument and his material. Thus he will be able to completely change the organism of music." It is essential, of course, that the composer work with the fullest spirit of love and service. Only then will he become the vehicle and the hand to lead back Music to her original throne.

Did you know that man will come to consider music as analogous to religion, mathematics and astronomy? As a result of the union of rational and spiritual, we will be able to give a new lease on life to the music of the ancients of Greece, India and Egypt. Only through the joining of sight, sound and understanding (which is the true meaning of the divine scale) will the plane of infinite harmonies throughout the immense orchestra of nature and the universe reach the soul and stir it to reproduce physical renderings of this tremendous orchestration. Man shall then lift himself to the heights of greater vision.

The tremendous qualities of brotherhood and service, as well as the will to create and to benefit mankind through the use of color and sound, will shimmer and shine in splendid colors throughout man's auric bodies. He will thus attract the mighty shining ones and through his language of color music, he will be able to speak. These masters or teachers or shining ones will, as a result, assist and teach the musicians and composers to understand their subtle forms of beautiful music.

These harmonies will be of great service to mankind. They will perform healing and creative missions in the many realms of nature. Thus there is a necessity for producing new instruments which should be capable of registering the finer subtleties of fractional tones, to which our outer ears as well as our nervous systems should be gradually accustomed. While in Europe I saw an instrument that looked like a conductor's baton. This was waved in the air, and music which equalled that of the human voice resounded from the ethers. This was completely an instrument of the new age.

Perfume, color and sound can be called the great Cosmic Tuning Fork. The prong which is perfume attunes our vehicles and recharges them through magnetism. In the future this will be used therapeutically and prophylactically. Perfume will play an important role in the treatment of dementia and

neurosis. Hence, perfume will lose her leading role as the ma-
donna of superficiality and will be removed from the boudoir
table with its label "Vanity." It will be lifted into the role of
"Service" and become one of the most subtle agents of vibra-
tional healing. Is this not easy to understand when the aromas
of our flowers and plant life are heaven-sent?

Therefore, in this evolving age we will move from the ancient tombs of kings the instruments of color, music and perfume. The temples of tomorrow will be fortified with this glori-
ously-awakened understanding of spiritual values and will act
as a sounding-board for all humanity.

In conjunction with these cosmic forces, we as individuals
have to lift ourselves consciously from the depths of ignorance
and prejudice. Only through our unfolding awareness will
there come an influx of power that is overwhelming. It will
transform our seven-fold bodies into living temples of radiance.
Our shining light shall act as a beacon to others who are on
the path and to those whose joy of expansion will help to light
the paths of others. Thus we find the flowering of a world-wide
service, radiant and positive in its well-being, which in its entirety of correspondences, will spell Brotherhood and Self-Real-
ization.

Chapter X

CHROMETHERAPY—
THE MEDICINE OF THE FUTURE

There is but one sickness and it is the root of all evil. Its name is "Congestion" or a block to the flow. Every time we, as individuals, block the flow of ideas and progress, we form "congestion" in society, and the symptoms are felt through wars and depressions. If it affects the mind, we call it ignorance or lack of high moral vibration. If it affects the physical body, it is termed "disease." The Christian Scientist calls it "error." No matter what we call it, it still means "congestion."

The body's way of recharging and restoring its forces is through the battery of higher vibration known as sleep. There are people who know how to recharge during the day, but the usual accepted form is sleep. Many people find it hard to fall asleep, and I would like to give those a little suggestion. First, recline on your back and relax. Think of the color cream-white, or imagine a yellow wall. Think this away. Make it disappear completely. Then let go. There you are in slumberland.

In order to progress we must daily add something new to our mental, physical and spiritual diets. It is not enough to know it, we must apply it. Thus we transfer the benefits from our spiritual bodies to the physical ones. Develop a keen sense of color consciousness or awareness. Acquire the habit of looking for color in all things. Take note of the subtle beauties and blendings which you have ignored and overlooked before. Make yourself consciously aware of color.

The man who first learns the French language finds that new doors open to him. When he goes to restaurants and orders from menus, he has more of an understanding as he recognizes the French words used to describe his favorite dishes. He thus becomes conscious of idioms and phrases that he has taken for granted in the past. So it is with color awareness. Once you learn the fundamental meaning of the color-significances, you will start applying it to the universe around you, and you will be amazed at the tremendous vistas that will open up to you.

There are a great many doctors who employ Chrometherapy. It is through these high-powered lamps behind colored slides that patients find relief and almost miraculous cures. The principle involved is simple, when understood, and works according to natural law. There was a sanitarium in Europe where they treated their patients only through color; they used color charged water and lamps.

The question is asked, "How can color cure?" The answer is not difficult to understand if you first realize that each human being creates a magnetic field around him which is known as the aura. It is the accumulation of the rates of vibration. Color Therapy works through this magnetic field. Each part of the body is controlled by a different color. Why? Because each organ has a different rate of vibration, and this is equivalent to a certain color. If there is a disease of that particular organ, there will be a low rating or a congestion. Color Therapy injects the rate of vibration through light or color into the body, thus tuning up the laggard organ.

To cure with Color Therapy is like tuning a violin. All health is dependent on the well-being and synchronized whole of all the organs. If one organ is not working well, the entire instrument is not functioning properly. In order to tune up the individual you must treat his weakest link.

Indigo blue, for example, is used for the lungs to remove congestion; it also stops ulceration and inflammation. Each color has a different application and meaning.

In the Worcester State Hospital they give color baths as a cure for those patients with mental diseases. A former Boston physician conducted an experiment with color and its effect on mental diseases. He said that colors are either stimulants or sedatives, and can be prescribed with beneficial results for individuals of normal mentality, as well as those of abnormal mentality. He explained that Nile green should be used as a spring tonic to tone up the system. Hence, the famous "green room" in the Worcester State Hospital. It is like a cavern at the bottom of the sea. The walls are painted light green, about the shade of a one cent postage stamp. There are green shades at the windows and the sunlight filters through them, producing a green light in the room.

There are four large bathtubs. These are the only furnishings. They are also green. After a few moments in this colorful atmosphere, complete tranquility descends on the patient, soothing his nerves rather than irritating them. The sensation inspired in this atmosphere is like that of a mountain glen on a hot summer's day.

Dr. William A. Bryan, superintendent of the Worcester State Hospital, who is well known for his experience and work at the Denver State Hospital and Boston Psychopathic Clinic, was questioned about the employment of colors in the treatment of certain mental diseases. I quote his answer, "I never took much stock in the therapeutic value of color until I had a personal experience that proved that there was something in it. During a sick spell which lasted about two weeks, I discovered that there was one room in my house where I could rest and sleep without suffering from nervousness and insomnia. This was a room with gray walls and gray furnishings. I felt the restful effect of this color from the moment I entered the room. This experience led me to believe that the potentialities of color as a medium in the aid of healing the sick seriously invited the consideration of the modern hospitals, especially those for mental diseases. Since that time, I have been investigating the subject, and I sincerely believe that the usefulness of color at the Worcester State Hospital has a very beneficial effect on the morale of the inmates, if nothing more."

We have found that the restful appearance of green walls and green light coming through the window shades has a most tranquilizing effect on agitated patients. We have also noticed that light green beds in the wards have a quieting effect on disturbed patients. We are doing away with white walls. We are painting bedrooms gray, light green and yellow in order to cheer the patients and give them a home-like environment.

It is interesting to note that the response excited by different colors conveys a definite impression to the mind. Generally speaking, scarlet and orange have the most exciting and emotional values, whereas yellow and green are the most soothing. Violet and purple are the most subduing in their effect. Once you establish the general direction of the reaction of the patient to these different hues, it becomes a comparatively simple matter to relate the desired responses with the proper conditions. By that I mean that if we find that a patient is melancholy and depressed we place him in an atmosphere that is stimulating. On the other hand, if the patient is nervous and excited, we apply sedative colors to him.

Red is a warm, aggressive color, combining the stimulating and forceful expressions of passion and fire. In laboratory experiments, when put under the influence of saturated red, the subject was shown to have muscular development fifty percent in excess of his usual physical prowess, when exposed to a more quieting hue. It is advisable, therefore, to use care in the use of red for decorative purposes. But we find that it is almost indispensible as an admixture to other colors in order to obtain a glow of warmth in a room.

We have used it effectively in combination with yellow, and with other colors in rooms where depressed and melancholy patients were temporarily placed. The bright cheerfulness of the yellow and the stimulating properties of the red combined, readily produced the desired emotions on the part of such patients, and they were soon conditioned to return to their own respective homes. Yellow, because of its high luminosity, suggests the life-giving qualities of the sun. It gives a room an agreeable atmosphere of brightness and warmth which is most desirable.

Blue, on the other hand, is colder than all the other hues. It exerts a depressing influence on most people. Gray is neutral, neither warm nor cold, neither stimulating nor depressing. It creates an atmosphere that is a happy medium between cheerfulness and gloom. Practically every normal individual reacts to color and the effect is immediately associated with the emotions. It is quite logical that those who are mentally diseased are even more susceptible to the color influence; in weakened states of health, the magnetic body of the individual reaches out and cries for help. Colors are the healers of nature—"the sedatives of the soul."

It might interest us all to realize that the primal cell of living matter is influenced by the vibratory activity of light rays. These are both visible and invisible. It is a crime against posterity to attempt to rear children without knowing more about color and its effect.

It distresses one to realize that the ignorance of colors should affect children as psychologically as it does. Children are dressed and surrounded in their nurseries with color vibrations that are either beneficial or detrimental to the health. Those

that are too stimulating are as sharp as a mustard plaster on
their little bodies. That accounts, often, for the acts of the
wayward child; they might often be traced to the improper
color saturation to which the little body was subjected in the
beginning of its life.

Through a study of colors and their characteristics, one can
determine the proper use of these light potencies under normal
conditions. If colors are to be used as correctives in abnormal
or subnormal conditions, a thorough knowledge of the leanings
and characteristics of the child must be known. In order to
apply the correct colors the mother better than anyone
else is able to help her child if she understands chromatic reactions and the herditary dispositional tendencies of her child.

If one is suffering from nervous hysteria one can easily say
that an external condition or mental influence in the life of the
individual has excited the nerves and mentality beyond control. I would suggest as a remedy, the slow restful environment of the blue vibration. Did you ever realize that environment is half of life?

If one suffers from anemia and is generally run down, a
gentle stimulation of the nerves is advisable. The red ray is
then the proper solution. It's not entirely satisfactory though,
except for very short periods. I don't advise supersaturating
the system with any one color.

It is absolutely necessary to have a thorough understanding
of the nature of colors in order to use them properly. This
holds good in the fields of decoration, architecture, medicine,
advertising or personal adornment. To use colors incorrectly
is like spilling poison. Colors radiate in all directions. If various colors are placed together, they vibrate and scintillate in
in every direction. It is both a duty and a task for the eye to un-
ravel this mass of vibrations and transmit them to the brain as
individual colors.

It is said on very good authority that 80% of the eye's work in the life of a human being is recharging the nervous system. Although the eye is designed for seeing and untangling the vibratory rates and translating them into colors, its mission in life is to pick up the healing vibrations that will balance the human instrument. If, however, the vibrations are so out of balance that their vibratory speed is unequal, they have a damaging effect upon the body. Therefore a pure red vibration, striking the body, has a very definite effect just as any other powerful, single color might have. However, if the vibrations are so combined that their speed is equal and hanging in proper balance, they can only be beneficial.

Sunlight is called white light. It is the element of normal growth and development. All colors are merely parts of white light—it is white light, broken up. Take a prism and hold it up to the light, and you will be both astounded and pleased at the galaxy of color which is portrayed. In understanding this you will realize that an unbalanced division of color, which either undercharges or overcharges the cells, has a very tangible effect on the human being. We are really like human batteries, and if we are to have an unbalance of color in our selves, we must resort to corrective measures such as light and color treatments. These should be given by trained color-scientists, and their relief is only temporary. I believe in correcting the disorder at its cause and removing it, rather than using this as a palliative. One must find the color disturbance in the environment and change it either in the surroundings or in the attire.

It is really not necessary to resort to spasmodic, intensified treatments, since color speeds bombard us every living minute of the day. It is, therefore, extremely important for our immediate surroundings and apparel to give us the necessary color treatments that we crave. Colors affect the emotions and they act as the language of our moods.

Every time you go out and behold a green tree, your eye, which sees only 20% of what is going on, uses 80% to re-charge the nervous system by catching the many shades and hues and tints of green which are present in every bough and in every leaf and translating them into the vibrations that feed the nervous system. God's greatest gift to man is the treasure with which he has sourrounded us—the wonderful beauties of nature. It is through the medium of color and this delicate sense-perception that we can transform this gift of color into a correct health-balance.

It is quite as necessary to have a correct color-diet as a food diet, since too much red or too much blue has a tendency to supersaturate the system with the vibratory element of one single color, which might be just as harmful as trying to live on one food. We have learned nowadays that instead of using colors in harmony as was practiced in the past, we use them for well-balanced contrasts. That is why this is called, "The Color-Age."

Human beings are like a violin. If each organ of the body is tuned to its proper rate of vibration, it sings the word, "Health." If there is one organ whose vibratory speed is below par, its song is, "Dis-Ease." Each rate of vibration is translated into a different color. For instance, we may say that the heart's vibratory rate is equivalent to that of red. The reason for this is that the structure and composition of this organ allows it to take from the white light every element except the rays which, when deflected, produce the vibratory sensation of the color red.

The liver, on the other hand, due to its different structure, is equivalent to another color, plum. If this organ is supplied with the white light which contains all the colorful elements in it, it draws its required needs and healthy activity is maintained.

The red ray, when found in surroundings such as the red dining-room, furnished nothing but that color from which the system can draw. Since the red ray is the only one present, and the heart uses all of the light rays except red, there would be a lack of supply of proper color-element for both the heart and liver.

The stomach being of another color, that would indicate that it absorbs a portion of several of the color speeds. This includes the red ray. There is, therefore, a tendency of over-saturation in this particular color-element. Since red is the color whose vibration is most favorable to fermentation, the digestive organ or stomach will suffer the consequences.

It is as bad to dress the body in red garments as it is to live in red environment. In the old days, it was customary for everyone to wear red flannels. This was known as the era of kidney disease. Red underwear was supposed to be warmer. Indeed, it was hot! This is true in more ways than one, since certain organs of the body are robbed of the necessary color elements. Their reaction, therefore, is a noticeable increase in the diseases of the kidneys. In those days they treated this disease of the kidney and liver as an ailment, but never received any permanent relief, since they did not perceive its cause.

The terrible period of wearing red underwear and eating in red dining rooms is passed. With it has gone the disease of the kidneys, and it hardly pays the patent medicine man to advertise his wares. Just to think that the proper knowledge and use of colors was the chief factor in bringing about this changed condition should sear itself upon our minds. It should make us aware that the necessity of a complete knowledge of colors is necessary if we are to enjoy a pleasurable life amid healthful surroundings.

Our age is the era of recognition of color principles. It is the age of sun-bathing. Because of recognizing the principle that all colors are in light, and that the body makes use of these colors, the bathing suit, which a century ago looked like a piece of armour, has been reduced to its present flimsy status. Many have said that the brevity of our modern bathing suits are in keeping with the moral laxity of our age, but they are wrong. The bathing suit was reduced because of scientific reasons. It is the greatest compliment to our age that we have recognized the fact that the human body requires more direct light and color in order to keep it balanced and healthy. This properly balanced color diet in our surroundings is one of the best guarantees of healthful living. Remember, colors may be only properly proportioned by balancing their vibratory speeds. For this we need a measuring rod, and that is the scientific scale.

During recent years, centers have been formed in western countries for the gathering up and giving out of esoteric knowledge of colors. There is Spectrochrome Institute in Malaga, New Jersey, with Dinshah P. Gadiahli and his spectrochrome philosophy, which teaches the treatment and cure of disease through the application of color. I studied with this great Zoroastian teacher, and found him most brilliant in his demonstration of vibrations. I witnessed some experiments that were breathtaking.

He took a large drum and on it he placed some sand. Then he took a violin and played it. The sound created vibrations in the air, and these in turn formed designs and patterns on the sand, thus showing the form of vibrations. His explanation of light through the spectroscope was equally interesting. He is undoubtedly the electrical wizard of our age.

I must not fail to mention one of the greatest color healers, Dr. Francis J. Kolar, formerly of Wichita, Kansas, and now living in Los Angeles.

While the science and art of diagnosis and analysis by color is not understood by the average person, it is practiced, however, by some of our greatest and advanced healers of the human race, such as Dr. Kolar. Science has at last found the pot of gold at the end of the rainbow by splitting up the spectrum. It has been shown that certain colors have healing qualities which rejuvenate our bodies and eliminate disease. Dr. Kolar performs bloodless surgery in more ways than one. He uses color in order to induce hypnosis. He performs operations which remove fibroid tumors and crystalline deposits without incision or pain, and with the patient in normal consciousness. He produces anesthesia or insensibility to pain by means of colored lenses or glasses which the patient wears. The lens of one eye is of a different color than the lens of the other eye. An electric light bulb is held about two feet above the head of the patient, and he is asked to look into it through the glasses to the count of ten, and then he is told to close his eyes for the same time. He continues doing this and becomes quite insensible to pain, although he is quite conscious and can converse intelligently with those around him.

In this way very delicate operations are capable of being performed for there is no necessity for any special preparation or any undesirable after effects from color-anesthesia. Dr. Kolar believes that the shock produced by ether or any other anesthesia is such a jar to the nervous system that it takes almost longer for one to recuperate from the effects of this than from the operation. The principle involved is that correctly prescribed colors promote the attunement to the higher bodies and that people do not remain aware of their physical body when perfectly attuned to those higher bodies. People that have developed color-consciousness are able to withdraw from pain.

If we recognize that through color we may slip from body to body or from plane to plane, we will know the secret of power.

Dr. Francis J. Kolar's color lenses induce this separation of the finer bodies, resulting in something entirely different from loss of consciousness such as is caused by the usual anesthetic. In the use of anesthesia we drive the conscious entity out of the body instead of isolating it. That is the key to future medicine and the open sesame of world relief.

There are many other color centers, such as Ivah Bergh Witten's, called The Aquarian Mystical Institute Of Color Awareness. This is located in Hollywood, California. She also has a branch in London, England. This is known as the Brighton Color Health Center. Its leader is Mrs. Farlough Smith. They work under the auspices of the International New Thought Association. Miss Witten's work is quite admirable and I feel that everyone should contact her work, since she teaches the spiritual side of color. There is also a Dr. Hanish at Mazdazdan in Los Angeles. The Theosophical Societies are also performing a broad and radiant service.

Lord Clifford of Chudleigh said, "Colors are not only effective to the cure of disease, but can add at least ten years to the life of a human being." He made this statement after he studied the action of light on vegetables and growths. He experimented with lights and noticed how the use of certain colors would stunt the growth of a plant while others would stimulate their growth. He finally came to the following conclusion: Yellow is the restorer of the nerves; Green increases the vitality of the nervous system; Red is effective in cases of blood poisoning; while Ultra-Violet produces a fermentation in the body, which reduces hardness of tissue. It also builds up blood cells. There is a certain shade of green which produces vitality and general energy in the system. . . . The greatest care should be taken that the right shade of each color is used. Yellow will only restore the nerves if the right shade is used. This holds good for all the colors, or else the results are opposite from those desired.

Pain is Mother Nature's warning. It is a signal, a sign and a friend. We might really term it the red light on the railroad track. Pain is Nature crying for help to remove the cause. I advise everyone to make a study of color and its therapy and learn to treat the cause of diseases, not only the symptoms.

A JOURNEY

TO THE

RAINBOW

A JOURNEY TO
THE RAINBOW

Light.

The greatest truth-teller and exposer of sham, showing up things the way they really are, is Light. It flows throughout the Universe and into our telescope, it descends into objects inconceivably small and even reveals through the microscope objects so tiny that they are invisible to the naked eye. Nature's finer forces usually have a wonderfully soft movement and yet they are so penetratingly powerful in their effect that they accomplish their purpose softly and wonderfully. Without Light, vegetables as well as animals would perish from the earth. It is therefore an interesting problem to consider as its potentialities are so great. The more deeply we penetrate into the inner laws, the more wonderful the store-house of power will reveal itself.

Nature, Our True Guide.

Why should Nature be the standard? Because we are all part of Nature and amenable to its laws. Secondly because Nature's laws are perfect. They bear the stamp of Divinity on them. No one can disparage Nature and love God. Every cause has an effect. Therefore if the cause is perfect the effect must be the same. In order to gain a knowledge of Nature's fine forces, we cannot use brilliant words and indulge in plausible speculation but we must build upon the perception of the divine harmony by which all of Science, Art, Government and Religion can be measured. That is the only way to know Nature's laws. Many writers, such as Ruskin, Chevreul of France, present in noble glimpses the real teachings of Nature. There are also many artists and scientific writers who reveal the rich lessons of this infinite treasure-house. However, it seems to me that some more definite crystallization of the principles of Nature's finer forces might be presented and as everything has already been presented to the world, the only thing I can do is to take you on a journey to the Rainbow where you will watch with me the dance of the electrons and the magnetons and you will listen to the steady heart-beat of the Universe. You are curious. So am I.

We are watching the Rainbow. It is smiling on the Universe with its eternal promise and we are intrigued.

"That is the promise that God has given to the world", said someone behind me. "Would you like to visit the Rainbow?"

So I found myself going to the Rainbow, which is really the place farthest out. The thought thrilled me. Perhaps I could catch a feeling that would enlighten me. It was like that dream farthest out that never quite materialized.

"There is something about the law of Unity which is universal. It is shown throughout Matter and Mind. It is really the expression of Oneness and of Organization.

Unity.

"Unity is a universal harmonic law. It exists in all unimpeded natural growth. In fact, all of Nature's development is based on the great law of Perfection. There are several methods by which Nature expresses this Unity.

The triangle is one of the examples. This is found in crystals and when the triangle is equilateral it has three points at the angles, thus three sides which all have a common center of

Unity. The hexagon has six points. This is also found in many crystals. Therefore it has twice as many points of Unity. The more the points of Unity, the more unlimited the expression of Nature's Unity. It is interesting that the minute skeletons of animals out of which whole mountains are sometimes built have so many points of Unity. The very circle is but a figure composed of an infinite number of straight lines which radiate from the same center and are equidistant. Thus if you will notice every leaf and other natural forms not only have centers of Unity in themselves but their very contour is apt to be a portion of another outline whose centers are outside of themselves."

With that long lecture on the subject of Unity I looked up at a tall, rather elderly man who probably was the Spirit of Unity. He moved towards me with a graceful glide and stopped.

"What do you think of what I just now told you?" he asked.

"I think," said I, "it is farther than I have taken any thought in all my life. If I were climbing a hill I would be puffing. I don't think I can follow you."

"Never mind", said he. "I'll show you." And with that he took up the leaves of the castor oil plant. "See", said he, "this presents one general center with seven sub-centers and still a larger number of small centers of Unity. The methods of Unity in the combination of leaves and trees and branches are beyond computation. I simply show you these," said he, "so that you can notice a great proof of all Nature proclaims."

I stared at my guide. Perhaps he was taking me to the Rainbow farthest out. Suddenly he paused and turned and looked at me.

"Pardon me, but are you a millionaire?"

"No," I replied, "I am just a Truth explorer. Why did you ask me?"

"Because," he replied, "you do not know your own heritage.

You do not know your Unity with Nature. If a tree has a trunk as its center of Unity, the branches sprout from the center and become centers within themselves for other smaller branches and thus they become less and less in size until each leaf becomes a miniature realm of itself, having organizations within organizations."

"You, as a human being are really a human system where thousands of centers of Unity found in the brain and spinal column act as general center of the nervous system."

"Well, if you want to get right down to it, I have noticed designs in snow-flakes and they might be the shapes such as the hexagon that you have mentioned before, but I never quite realized that when Nature is unrestricted it always moves according to the laws of Unity."

"Of course," said he, "we might make an experiment right here." With that he took a violin from under his arm. He then asked me to sprinkle some dry sand on a flat surface. He started to play the violin and lo and behold but the sand began to develop principles of Unity showing triangles, circles, hexagons, in fact all designs. I was very enthusiastic as here was proof of Nature's freest operation as developed according to law. What law? It must be some mathematical law of Unity.

"You see," said he, "even verse and musical compositions have a Unity in the length of their steps and this is called Rhythm, whereas Melody demands some ruling tone, and this is called Key Note. This is the trunk of the tree around which the other notes cluster. All light emanates in untold millions of rays from the center of Unity called the Sun. Therefore all colors combine in a wonderful Unity to form white light and even when they are separated by a prism or by the Rainbow, they blend so perfectly as seemingly to be but one single band of colors."

"One thing I can't understand", said I. "What holds or binds this Universe into this one law? What force makes all objects go towards the central point?"

"Good!" said he. "That remark pleases me. It shows that you are starting to think. You are really bordering the Rainbow. The answer is Gravitation. It is the law of cohesion. This law deals with atoms. It binds up solids into a firm Unity of mass and rolls up fluids into little tiny spheres, each of which has again a center. Gravitation, however, is really the family binder because it takes all the masses of atoms and chisels out the world into their beautiful globular shapes and then ties them together. Thus the Sun becomes the center of Unity of one hundred and thirty-seven planets, and that sun is but a mere point in the vast reach into space as there are many, many more suns far beyond our speculation. The Milky Way which William Herschel found was composed of 18,000,000 stars, is but a center around which other immense clusters make their infinite circuit. Otherwise how could they be held in such a mass yet separated from the rest of the Universe?"

"I know the answer", said I anxiously. "It is the same principle. It is the law of Unity plus the law of Gravity which is the binder which keeps things in their splendid order. It is marvelous that this law of Unity and these thousands of star clusters, each of which is almost a Universe in itself, can be manifested into one Almighty Center which we might call God."

"You are right," said my friend, "all analogies would fail and all attempts to arrive at a universal law are but sheer mockery if we did not see this wonderful principle of Unity. No matter where we look for it, we will find that it is absolutely universal."

"Wonderful, this explains Matter to me," said I.

"Yes, but the Unity of the material universe is not everything," replied my friend. "There is the supposition that Spirit is unlike Matter. That would mean that there would be no bonds of Unity between Spirit and Matter and Spirit could never act without Matter, nor could Matter act without Spirit. I wish it could be understood that the very same law which rules in the spiritual and intellectual phases of being are also shown in the material."

"I see," said I hastily. "You mean there is a Unity of principle which rules in every department of life and binds everything into one."

"Yes," smiled my friend. "Mankind understands this intuitively and expresses this constantly in such phrases as 'Heat of fire,' or 'Light of Knowledge,' or 'Harmony of Colors,' or 'Sound,' or 'Harmony of Feeling.' "

"You mean our words express the inner feeling of our processes?"

"Yes," said my guide, "there is a chemical affinity ruling the psychological and ethereal forces which are just as absolute as those that work in the psychological and ordinary material conditions. Unity is found in all realms of Matter and Force."

"I see. In other words, all things basically speaking resemble all other things. We therefore can judge the unknown by the known and the invisible by the invisible, and the whole by its part."

"Yes," assented my friend. "This is the greatest and the most important law and gives us the key to all the mysteries. But it makes us wonder what other law which is equally important is necessary to harmonious Unity."

"Do you mean to say that there *is* another law?"

"Yes, there is the law of Diversity."

"Let me introduce you to my friend who represents this law just as I represent the law of Unity."

I was silent and when I turned my eyes in the direction of my friend Unity I found that he had left me. I could still see and feel the abandoned relaxation of his walk and talk and then as I turned and looked up I could see a man walk towards me. For a moment I thought that he was Unity but no sooner had this thought crossed my brain when I heard his voice say:

"I am the Spirit of Diversity, which is the Law of Nature which exemplifies Freedom, Life, Individuality and Infinity. I would like to show you how there is Unity in Diversity."

"Oh," I sighed. "This is going to be very complicated."

"Not at all," he smiled. "What a perverted style of Unity it would really be if the triangle would not move in three directions or the hexagon in six directions. There is Diversity in all. There is even Diversity in Light and Shade. There is Diversity in Form and in Color."

"I understand. That is why trees have such diversity in their direction and their size and their leaves, their barks, their flowers, their fruit. In short, everything from Man to the Sea, to the Sky, to the Earth, is rich only because of the infinitude of the forms, the sounds, the colors and the motions which it takes. This is again shown in the world of Literature and Spiritual Power when used with Diversity.

"Harmony, you see, consists of an equal balance between Unity and Diversity. The exquisiteness of this Harmony is increased in proportion to the number of parts of the Unity and Diversity."

"That is a bit too deep for me."

"Not at all. Think about it," he said. "If the whole world were black all the time, it would be very uninteresting because there wouldn't be any Diversity. It is because of the Light and the Shade that the world becomes interesting. Colors must combine a variety of tints, hues and shades in order to please. If we should see a daub of color on an object without any Unity of law in its arrangement, our taste would be offended because it would be Diversity run wild, whereas if we would see only one color it would become most boring and insupportable. Or if we should see Light and Shade mingled in a lawless mass we would be most distressed. It would be somewhat like a barren, treeless desert, or an absolute dark mass of ruins. It is the relief which in turn gives the freedom and the law of Unity combines with this and delights our eyes."

"How interesting! I believe that Joshua Reynolds tried very hard to make one-third of his pictures shadow and two-thirds light."

"Yes, but that is not the rule. If light or shade predominates too much the diversity is not sufficient to balance the unity, and the objects are less distinct than they would be if the balance were more harmonious. All real artists feel that light and shade must be exactly balanced as is shown in nature, where the nights and days have the same average length, and where the positive and the negative forces must be evenly balanced in order to make smooth and perfect action."

"Is that why as soon as there is too much cold or heat people get out of balance?" I asked.

"Yes. The two principles, heat and cold must be evenly balanced. Heat is the principle of Diversity, an outward expansion, whereas cold is the principle of Unity or organization and crystallization. Both together make a harmony. But when used separately they act destructively," answered my friend.

"That's true. But lots of times, when principles are combined, they are very good. How do you account for the sweetness and acidity in fruits? They are opposites." I questioned.

"Yes. Sweetness and bitterness are often combined such as in tea and coffee. Sweetness and acidity are combined in fruits, such as strawberries and peaches and lemons. But they are a balanced combination of Unity and Diversity, so equally distributed that they seem to reach and delight the esthetic taste, as in the beautiful or sublime. They set into motion the harmonious flow of those forces and senses which makes us call them delicious—our taste buds," answered my friend.

"These basic principles can be applied to every department of life, both in mind and matter?" I anxiously asked.

"Why not? Nature's great love is shown in various ways," answered Diversity.

"I have not thought of it quite in that way," I answered reflectively.

"Then think again. What is gradation but the delicate degree of progression from one condition or quality to another condition or quality. Take a sunset for instance. When you move from East to West, you will find that the gradation of colour is towards a superior brilliancy, whereas when you move from West to East, there is a drive for softness in colour. The rainbow is the very best example of a harmonious blending of colours or progression towards superior fineness. It is the rainbow which moves from red to orange, yellow, green, blue, indigo and violet. It moves from coolness to warmth of life," answered friend Diversity.

"I see. If there were contrasts instead of gradual gradations, things would not be very graceful," I answered thoughtfully.

"Have you ever thought that the human limbs and features are about the best example of the principle of gradation; the great love of Nature is shown in this principle in all of the trees. Take the beech tree. It has a round topped head, whereas the poplar has an oblong head. The beech tree, because of using too little diversity in its progression, towards the point, gives more of a stiff appearance than the sparry-topped trees such as the cedars, firs and larches. These trees are more attractive than either the beech or the poplar because they make greater use of the principle of diversity and angles and forms, and present sharp contrasts which are striking, as well as subtle fine gradations."

"Do you know that I never thought of all that. Who would

ever think of trying to group Nature the way you have done!"
I exclaimed.

"What is more, there is a gradation of direction as well, you
see there is more to the principle of Diversity of gradation.
There is Diversity of direction. When there is gradation of direction, there is beauty of form, because curves are then evidenced, and they are the leading features of beauty in forms."

"Oh, I had never thought that there are different kinds of
curves, but then on second thought, there must be," I replied.

"Yes, there is the curve called parabola. This you find in
the curves that fountains make. It is also found in cataracts.
The English artist Hogarth named a curve which was un-
dulatory in its movement, the Line of Beauty. This you find
in the meandering of a stream. It is so prevalent in nature,
when you look at the undulating of the grass swaying in the
wind, or if you look at leaves, flowers, stream or shells, you
will find this line of beauty or undulating effect. Hogarth named
another line which was spiral. He called this the Line of Grace.
This you find in climbing vines in curls of the hair, as well as in
sea shells. It's the most beautiful of all simple and continued
lines, and yet the most common in the Universe. The vibration
of sounds when recorded by a graphic instrument, has also
gradation of size and direction."

"I know that EDWIN BABBIT, the greatest thinker, and who
wrote the "Principles of Light and Colours," said that when you
place a sponge of an electrical machine to the left eye and make
the current strong enough, you see stars or rings which vibrate
from the ends growing weaker as they approach the centre
where they seem to die out. He said that it starts with yellow,
and then about at the fourth or fifth ring it becomes red, and
then disappears into faint blue," I answered.

"Very good indeed," answered my friend. "You will know
then that these waves of light that you have spoken about prog-

ress in colour, in size and in direction, and according to their line of beauty, always showing a unity, while the features of diversity are equally expressed. The human form is really the highest development of the external universe and therefore should manifest the highest of harmonic features. Have you ever thought that when a child is very young its head is round, and then as it matures, its head becomes oval. The Romans thought that the circle was the highest form of beauty, while the Greeks preferred the oval. They said that the circle was stiff, whereas there was more variety in the oval.

"There is a constant progression whether it is from one form to the other or one colour to the other or one motion to the other or one sound to the other. Fundamentally there is a constant drive towards superior gradations showing the unity of law which exists in the world of intellect and language as well as external nature. This gradation is a universal law and extends to gravitation and chemical affinity as well," answered friend Diversity.

This journey to the Rainbow is like a dream, a dream that I had yearned for for many years. It was an explanation of these various laws about me that I had always wondered about. Yet I was still curious. Up till now I had always been content with what my eyes had shown me and with what people had told me. But suddenly I realised that the greatest things are the invisible things that the eye does not see and the ear does not hear. And while gazing out into space I heard a voice say: "I am the invisible light behind things. I am called Odic light and I will be glad to tell you about myself."

I waited, filled with curiosity.

"Every colour has a certain style of power, no matter how fine or coarse it might be. The Odic colour has the same characteristics as the visible colours. Every colour works under the same law. The only difference is that the colours of a finer

grade have a softer and more penetrating power than the colours
of the coarser grade. They also have a greater influence on the
finer mental forces as well as the physical forces of man. Blue
and violet are cool in nature. They are electrical, while red is
warm and exciting."

"But what is Odic light and colour really? Is it nature? I
don't understand." I questioned.

"The Odic light shows the same laws and has exactly the
same phenomena as the ordinary light, and must work in connection with a fine atmosphere of its own, just as common light
works in connection with the atmosphere we breathe. Odic force
emanates from all objects, and manifests itself in the form of
a light, when these objects are kindled into action by the sunlight, moonlight, electricity, heat, magnetism or friction."

"Is that why I see sparks when I walk across a carpet, or is
that what makes glow-worms glow?" I questioned anxiously.

"Professor Endlicher was able to see odic flames at the end
of a magnet. He blew on the odic flame at the end of this magnet
and produced an actual flame, just like an ordinary flame that
flickers in the wind."

"Well, what is the cause of this phenomena?" I queried.

"The cause of this phenomena is a peculiar force existing in
nature and embracing the universe, distinct from all known
forces, and called Odyl. There are many people who are called
Sensitives and they are able to perceive these odic or invisible
lights. The greatest man to experiment in this field was Baron
Reichenbach, who was one of the most eminent scientists of
Austria. He made the discovery that the fine forces which issue
from all known elements and substances appear in beautiful
lights and colours which can be both seen and felt by persons
called sensitives. In a beautiful castle near Vienna, he insti-
tuted thousands of experiments which extended over many
years, and which were conducted with a severe love of truth

which will always make his name immortal. He named this subtle power OD, or Odic force, or Odylic force. These fine invisible emanations constitute the basic principles of all other forces and are forever working through all things. Professor Tyndall said that if we allowed ourselves to accept for a moment that notion of gradual growth and ascension implied by the term called evolution, we might fairly conclude that there are stores of visual impressions awaiting man far greater than those he is now in possession of. Ritter discovered that beyond the ultra-violet there are a vast number of rays which are absolutely useless to us because of our present power of vision. It is interesting however, that people can develop the vision to see the odic lights," said my companion, with a smile of understanding and a knowing look on his face.

"What a wonderful world we are living in and what tremendous possibilities! I feel as though I have not lived until this moment. I am so intrigued to know more. What do you suppose would happen if everybody could see the odic light?" I questioned anxiously.

"That, my dear, is the promise of the future when mankind will develop and will not only be able to see the moonlight on the water but will hear a heavenly symphony that is being played by the universe continuously. Every mountain has its music, every form has its tune, every colour has its own keynote. What a wondrous universe! What a promise for the future!" answered my companion.

"How is it that the world does not know about this force which promotes human happiness and is so up-building?" I again questioned.

"Berzelius, the great chemist from Stockholm, and Dr. Elliotson, president of the Royal Chirurgical Society of London and Dr. Gregory of the Edinburgh College, all found this great force. Their praise of Baron Reichenbach's discovery was unlimited.

However, there are still too few who know about it," answered my teacher.

"Tell me about some of the experiments he made so that I can tell the world about it," I replied.

"It is said on very good authority that Madame Kienisberger awakened in the middle of the night and thought that her iron window frame had caught fire. Large flames devoured the window frame. This was not a case of an optical illusion, but an actual case of seeing odic light. She was a sensitive, and used by Baron Reichenbach for his experiments. When she would lie quietly she would see lights that would not appear when moving about interrupting her finer vision," answered my friend Odic Light.

"Is this a force that can be felt at a distance, or does one have to be very close to it in order to sense it," I asked.

"No, it is interesting that odic light can be felt through several rooms. That is the odic force of magnets, crystals and human bodies. You see, odic light has the same law of refraction and reflection as any ordinary light, but at the same time it is able to pass through opaque bodies and make them transparent. Baron Reichenbach made an interesting experiment showing that odic light was not dependent on our atmosphere, but completely independent of it," said my teacher.

"How would he ever be able to do that?" I questioned wonderingly.

"He took the magnet and then put it in a Bell jar. He then withdrew all the air with an air pump. He had as witnesses those who were sensitives, such as Madame Kienisberger and a man called Johann Klaiber and a Mr. Firke. When the air was half removed from the jar, the magnet began to show an odic glow. After that with every stroke of the piston the flame became greater until it overflowed the Bell jar. As soon as air was admitted, the odic lights disappeared. This was seen by all three witnesses. When the air had been removed from the jar, both ends of it glowed brightly. One pole was red and the other blue. This was distinctly seen by a sensitive called Mlle. Zinkell. You wonder what this proves. Simply this, that some day we will harness this force and be able to light up our streets with this cold odic light. It might even drive our machinery. Therefore it behoves all scientists and searchers of the truth to try to find out more about it," said my companion with a generous smile.

"How wonderful! This is a real challenge and a call to all thinkers to marshall their forces and enlist in this search. But how does one know if one is a sensitive?" I queried anxiously.

"That is simple. I will make an experiment with you." And with that he drew a very large magnet from his pocket.

"I will pass this magnet from your head to your toes, and if you are a sensitive you will feel a very marked pull. That accounts for some people not being able to sleep when the moon is shining on them. You see the magnet is not the only way that nature presents this magnetic reaction. The earth itself is an example of this magnetism as well as all the crystals which act in line of their axes. The true cause of this phenomena is the odic force," said my teacher coming towards me, and passing the magnet over me. I instantly felt as though flames were coming out of me, and then and there I could understand how according to Professor Endlicher, flames as high as forty inches in height could rise out of a magnetic steel magnet surrounded with beautiful colours from red and yellow to blue."

"How wonderful!" said I, "but is the human being the only source that can give out these odic lights?"

"Why, no," answered my companion, "Miss Sturman found that a large rock crystal gave out flames half the size of a hand from blue passing to white. The difference between this and the magnetic light is that it has no red or yellow in it. Crystals, it was discovered, present two poles, one pole acting more strongly than the other gives forth a cooler current, while the other a warmer current. There are different grades of heat and cold, but the cold end of the crystal gives out a blue light, while the warm end a red wave. According to Baron Reichenbach, the north end of a crystal or magnet is the blue ray or negative pole, while the south end is the positive and red pole. He discovered that the right side of a human being emits the blue ray or negative force, while the left side gives out the red or positive force," said my companion.

"Where does the power of the magnet come from?" I questioned.

"The power of the magnet comes from the electrical currents arranged in curves, thus giving it its power. It's the flow of this odic force that gives each thing its identity. Take plants and trees. They are usually warm at the lower end and cold at the upper extremity. This is because the odic current runs that way. Did you know that every metal and alkaline substance was either warm or cold too?" asked my companion.

"I had not thought of that. But that should be very interesting. Tell me about it," I pleaded.

"Every metal and alkaline substance is warm, and according to sensitives, every acid was found to be cold. The coldest substance, next to oxygen, is sulphuric acid and water. Mlle. Reichel, a sensitive, saw most metals as red, almost red-hot. There were few metals that gave off a white light, whereas others gave off a yellow light, and copper was found to give off a green light. Baron Reichenbach told Mlle. Reichel to hold the end of a wire thirteen yards long which was connected to plates which were placed in the sun-light. She was told to hold the wires up, and as she did so, in less than a minute, a stream of light about ten to twelve inches, emerged. When various other metals were used after being charged in the sunlight, the flames that ensued were from green to blue found in copper, clear white from gold and silver, whereas dull white came from tin, and reddish white from zinc," said my companion.

"That just shows you that the power of the sun can recharge, doesn't it?" I answered, very much impressed by what I had heard.

"Yes, the healing power of the sun does not only come from the visible colours, but from the odic colours, which form the next colour octave above the visible range. For instance a blue glass transmits a larger amount of odic rays than a yellow or orange glass. But then there is the influence of moonlight as well as sunlight," he continued. "Sensitives found that the current of the moon was warm, and when they looked at the plates charged with moonlight holding up the wire, such as they did with the former experiment, they saw flames ten inches in length arising. Dr. Forbes Winslow in his great work called "Influence of Light," show that in warm climates diseases are more acute during the time of the full moon than at any other time. In fact, he says that death has often occurred from a stroke of the moon, and blindness in Egypt has been found in people who have fallen asleep with their faces expcsed to the intense moonlight. The blue glass or a blue veil is a great saviour in these instances, as the blue offsets the exciting influence of the moon. The moon is harmful only in negative conditions of sleep. Dormant conditions however, are benefited by the moonlight and walking in the open moonlight brings only benefit and not harm."

"The thing that puzzles me is what is the difference between magnetism and odic light. How can one tell the difference?" I questioned.

"That is a very intelligent question. I shall try to answer it. The odic light can be developed without the aid of magnetism, whereas magnetism cannot be without odic force. All bodies are charged with odic force, just a few humans are charged with magnetism. The odic force cannot attract iron filings, whereas a magnet does. Magnetism lingers on the surface of bodies, whereas the odic force penetrates into the bodies, often making them transparent. The magnetism is much coarser from odic light in many ways. The poles of a magnet or of a crystal, and the ends of the fingers are charged with odic force. The proof that odic light is not imaginary is that every sensitive describes it in the same way, and can point out any object that has been charged with odic force, even water. One of the experiments that Baron Reichenbach made to show that the odic force or magnetism could be sensed, was that he took a sensitive called Miss Nowotny and put her in a cataleptic state. Immediately her hands were drawn to a magnet near by. Baron Reichenbach himself went into the next room and opened up a magnet of ninety pounds sustaining power. The effect on the sensitive was one of great restlessness and uneasiness. She kept murmuring that she was having pain, that a magnet was open. As soon as Baron Reichenbach removed the magnet, her pain disappeared. According to Edwin Babbitt, M. Baumgartner, professor of physics, held up to the sensitive a magnet deprived of its magnetism, and she immediately discerned it."

"Are these forces of magnetism and OD also found in the earth?" I asked.

"Yes indeed," answered my teacher. "Baron Reichenbach made some very ingenious experiments to show that the odic force was really the cause of the Aurora Borealis. There is a difference between the Northern Lights that can be seen by the ordinary eye and the odic light which because of its intensity cannot be seen by ordinary vision. He took a magnet and placed it in a hollow iron globe with the north and south poles in correspondence with the north and south poles of this globe. He then found that blue was sent forth from the north, and red from the south, much the same as the Aurora Borealis appears. He showed how magnetism on a small scale could develop such colours in connection with the odic atmosphere, thus illustrating how the greatest play of the world's mightiest concentrated magnetism at the poles might ignite the ordinary coarser atmosphere with its nebulous matter, and so cause a similar effect to the vision of man."

"Do the sensitives see any colours at different points of the earth?" I asked.

"Yes, at the North Pole a brilliant light ascends which merges into delicate horizontal colours such as red, yellow, green and blue. The South Pole is stronger in its electrical currents, and therefore red and yellow predominate. One might easily say that the horizontal forces of the earth are electrical, therefore blue, which is in the direction of the North Pole, and east of the North Pole is indigo, then violet, then blue-green, and lastly in the east, where there is just a feeble electricity, there is a slight bluish grey. In the south the colours are thermal such as red, and in the west, yellow forces predominate, and north of the west, south-west and south-east, there is orange, red-grey, and yellow-green. Because of these various forces, there is naturally an effect upon all living bodies on the earth, and therefore, these great forces of the earth can be beneficially applied to harmonize with the constitution of man."

"Do you mean that we have the same radiations in our own bodies as the earth has? Therefore, should we apply our directions in correspondence with the earth's directions?" I asked.

"Yes, it is important to observe the forces of the earth flowing harmoniously with those of the human body. Therefore it is important that in sleeping, the head should be towards the north in order to receive the blue or violet currents, and the feet being colder towards the south, to receive the warm currents, such as the red and the orange. It is amazing how sensitive patients respond to the right direction, and when they lie in direction contrary to the harmonious flow of nature's finer forces, such as south-north or west-east position, no matter what the medicine used might be, it is powerless to have an effect in this perverted position. Many a medical man has made countless blunders because of ignoring these facts. It would be wise, before asking people to change the position of their beds, to explain to them that the cold magnetic forces of the earth, as they move northward, give the magnetic needle its direction, and the head being charged with blood, it needs this cooling element," said my companion.

"If there is a position for sleeping, there must also be a position for sitting," I asked.

"Yes, indeed, there is. It is much better to sit with one's back to the north or north-east or at least to the east, in preference to any other direction, especially when taking a sun-bath, or any other kind of treatment," answered my teacher.

"Is that why it is often very painful for me to sit for a length of time in certain places?" I asked wonderingly.

"Yes. That is especially true in some churches which are built from west to east so that the congregation finds itself opposite the altar in the position of west to east. This is intolerable for some sensitive creatures as it is the direction counterindicated for the human body," answered my friend.

"Could it possibly be that ignorance of this law might affect members with nervous symptoms in our families?"

"Yes indeed. They could be attuned to the beautiful radiations of light and nature's finer forces. They might sleep in a direction not exactly north-east, but some thirty degrees east of north, enabling them to receive the strong and cool northward current of the head and upper body. But, universally speaking, the north-south position is better, especially in such countries as England and France. Whereas the east of the north position of the head would be excellent for people of the Pacific states, and some states farther east. The ideal would be for residences to be built on avenues running from north to south, so, that the sun may purify both sides of the house," said my companion.

"Would not plant life also be affected?" I asked.

"Yes, if one would take a wire and put it in the earth of the flowerpot, and connect the other end to some pipe that enters the earth, the growth of the plant would become accelerated to a much larger degree than the plant that has no connection with the terrestial forces. This same principle might be applied to man. If a copper wire is connected to the bed of the sleeper, and the other end is attached to a radiator whose pipe enters the earth, there is a constant flow of magnetic forces played upon the individual, just as though he were sleeping on the ground. This is known as terrestial dynamics," stated my companion.

This was the realization of my dream farthest out. These were explanations of the things I had been thinking and wondering about for many years. And now I had found the key to the lock. I could hardly believe my luck, and as I looked up to thank my companion, I found that he had disappeared, and the only thing that remained of his presence was the heart pulse of these thoughts that he had set into action. I felt quite lonesome, when I heard a voice say: "I am a colour healer, I am the healing power of all colour."

"The healing power of all colour, I've never heard of that!" I exclaimed.

"Minerals are at the bottom of Nature's scales of force. They are so crude that these particles are unable to float in the atmosphere, and therefore they are deposited in the earth. Since vegetables constitute the direct food of man, they are but siftings of the coarser mineral elements by the ingenious process of the sun, while the elements that come from the earth are strained of their coarser ingredients by the spongioles of the roots, and absorbed in a liquid state. That is why cereals and fruit that grow above the ground, and drink in the refined elements of the sun, constitute a higher grade of food than those that grow in the ground, such as roots, tubers, radishes, potatoes and onions. Pure air furnishes more of a material combination of elements than water, as it includes those that are volatile to float, and presents those finer ethers which are constantly in action during the daytime while the sun shines. Water combines various grades of electricity, but the finest power of all is sun-light, being of a psycho-magnetic radiation. By understanding these powers and these laws we see how all things must radiate their own peculiar ethers, whereas they must also partake of the substances through which they pass, therefore reflecting the finest substances which have the finest emanations," said my new companion.

"Is there a special meaning for the various colour rays?" I asked curiously.

"Yes indeed. The power of the red ray is to stimulate the arterial blood. This is shown in cases of healing with the red light. You see, red stimulates and increases the action of the warm red principle in the human system. It harmonises the cold blue principle which is the cause of paleness of countenance and blueness of the veins. Because there is the law of unity that reigns throughout nature, drugs have a wave-length, and those of the red wave-length must produce the same results as the red light. The same principle in sun-light and everywhere else must produce similar results. The only difference between sun-light and drugs is that the elements of sun-light are more penetrating than the coarser elements of the drugs," answered my companion.

"That certainly is deep for me. I can't imagine any drug being red. Could you name some?" I queried.

"Everything that has a burning prickly sensation when swallowed has some of the red principle in it. There is cayenne pepper which is a powerful stimulant, produces heat in the stomach and a glow over the body. It is an arterial stimulant. There is the Balsam of Peru which is a warm stimulating tonic. Cloves are the most stimulating of aromatics. Bromine is caustic and irritant, is also a red liquid. Iron has a reddish cast and acts as a powerful tonic raising the pulse. Red cedar which is a stimulant is a diuretic. Musk is stimulant and anti-spasmodic. It increases the vigour of the circulation. Ammonium carbonate is powerful in the red principle of hydrogen and acts as an arterial stimulant. Alcohol where red predominates strongly is a stimulant of hardened arteries. Oxygen develops the red principle of the blood. The power of red glass has been found to have worked wonders in the case of despondency," said my companion.

"Yes, but what you have given me are the names of drugs, but you have not told me what red light can do."

"That is simple. The red light, like red drugs, is the warming element of sunlight, and arouses the nerves as well as the blood, especially when the light is applied through various grades of red glass. This is found to be excellent in cases of paralysis and other dormant conditions, says Dr. S. Pancoast. There was a young boy aged eight, who in recovering from diphtheria, was suddenly struck by paralysis. His condition was very bad as he could not walk, and could only stand when supported. Upon being placed in red light baths for from one to two hours daily, he would fall asleep, and start to perspire. In two months he was perfectly well," said my teacher.

"This is indeed a new world for me. Tell me some more, some other stories like the last one."

"Well, there was a lady whose knee was bent and ankylosed by rheumatism. She had baffled the doctors for many months. The knee was cold as a piece of dead flesh, and only upon the application of red light was the blood made to kindle new life in that part. She was then placed in a solar sweat bath, and lo and behold after the second treatment, her leg was straightened out. So you see, the red light is a friend to rheumatism as well as paralysis, consumption and physical exhaustion. Edwin Babbitt, the greatest worker in the field of light and colour, has explained these cases to the world. There was the case of a woman who was in the last stages of consumption, and Dr. Pancoast placed this lady under red baths, and in two weeks improvement began to show, and in the third week the condition began to improve and soon respiration had resumed throughout the left lung, the negative condition in the right lung disappeared and her strength had increased. Dr. Pancoast claimed he had never heard of a case of consumption that could not be helped no matter what stage it was at. Then there is the case of physical exhaustion. A man who was overworked, and whose mind and body were continuously out of harmony, who could neither sleep nor eat, finally suffered from nervous prostration. He was given the red light treatment, and the results were really remarkable. The first bath he took acted as a tonic on his mind and body, and finally, as the light doses were increased, he regained his strength and returned to business. It took three weeks' treatment for this cure to be effected."

"If the red ray is so good, why doesn't everyone take it all the time?" I questioned.

"The red ray can be injurious when there is already too much red, or when there is an inflammatory condition. Red haired people as well as those whose countenances are florid or feverish, must take very little red. Iron is contra-indicated in inflammatory conditions. It is interesting that the red ray has a very exciting effect on people as well as on animals. An experiment was tried in a French insane asylum on some violent and maniacal patients, who were placed in a room with a red ray. The symptoms of these patients became more violent, and so they had to be removed and placed in a room where the blue ray predominated. They immediately became calm and quiet, and would almost fall asleep. You see, it takes the skilful physician to use the red glass, because one must take a precaution that when the system becomes too hot, that a blue glass must be put in place of the red glass or a bandage must be placed on the head. In cases of lethargy, it is better to have a blue glass on the head and a clear glass over the rest of the body."

"How wondrous all this seems. What would happen to the yellow and orange rays, and what is their healing effect?" I asked.

"Good for you. Yellow is especially good for the nerves. The drugs whose yellow principle works somewhat more slowly do not exert their action until they reach the intestines, where they act as a purgative. And those drugs that have an affinity for the liver and bile, act as Cholagogues, and those that stimulate the kidneys are Dietics. Those which stimulate the nerves of the skin are called Diathoretics. They make the skin perspire. Those which bring the blood to the skin are called Rubefacients. In all of these cases yellow is the principle of nerve stimulus as well as the exciting principle of the fountain head of the nerves which is the brain. When elements excite the brain they are called cerebral stimulants. You might be interested to know some of the drugs and foods which belong to this category."

"Oh yes. That would be most enlightening and useful. I am beginning to realize that I have never translated the meanings of the very things around me."

"That is right. That is why I have come to visit you and show you the healing power of the light rays of this universe, and how light becomes solidified in these various drugs and foods. The following are some emetics which have a good deal of the yellow, red and orange wave in them. They are called Indian Hemp, Lobelina, Tartar Emetic, Blood root. All emetics deal so much in the red as well as the yellow principle, that they act on the blood and muscular tissues as well as on the nerves. The laxatives and purgatives are May Apple, Senna, Colocynta, Capaiba, Gluten, Figs, magnesia, magnesium carbonate, castor oil, olive oil, sulphur, magnesium sulfate, prunes, Cape Aloes."

"But that does not show me the healing power of the yellow light. Tell me some instances."

"There was a case of bronchial irritation which when treated with a yellow light over the breast, inside of a minute, was able to show results. Finally, after twenty minutes each day during several days, the condition cleared up. Then there was a case of costiveness where Dr. Babbitt let the sunlight pass through a yellow glass, and focused it on the intestinal track, especially over the descending colon. After ten minutes, perspiration broke out over the entire body, and five minutes afterwards the bowels commenced to resume their peristaltic action, and thus a case of costiveness was cured."

"What would happen if one would mix two colours together?" I asked.

"When you mix yellow with red, you have such drugs as dandelion, pure carbonate of calcium, potassium nitrate, sassafras oil, Seneka, Buchu, oil of Savene, and mustard. There are also those cerebral stimulants such as opium, Saffron, Valerian, Ether. There are a few tonics with a yellow and red predominant. Tonics are substances which invigorate the human system. Some of the best tonics have a fair share of electrical colours.

Quinine and iron are the most important tonics. There is also a tonic called Quassia, Gold Thread, Gentiane, Peruvian Bark, Iron, Myrrh Ginger and black pepper."

"Yellow is so good for one, I shall proceed to use it all the time," I volunteered.

"Yellow, when aided by some orange and red is the central principle of nervous excitement. Yellow is specially predominant in laxatives and purgatives, and when combined with red and orange forms the leading element in cerebral stimulants. Yellow is injurious in all over-active nervous conditions, such as delirium, sleeplessness and diarrhea. Yellow is the most decided principle in poisons. The nerves of the insane are irritated by yellow, and one must remove the yellow shade in those asylums. One great reason why yellow rules in the most violent of poisons such as prussic acid and strychnine, is because of the prominence of the yellow principle as a stimulus of the nerves combined with the red principle as a stimulus of the blood. Because the yellow principle is so powerful in its action on the nerves, we may easily understand why large doses of yellow drugs are said to cause convulsions and delirium, as well as other symptoms. Even so mild a substance as coffee with its yellow-brown principle is said to be contra-indicated in acute inflammatory affections, causing a disposition to wakefulness. Those who wish to escape some of the worst effects of coffee should not let it steep more than five to ten minutes, when the coffee grounds should be removed from the liquid thus preventing the tannin from escaping. The tannin is the astringent principle in coffee, whereas coffee alone has a laxative effect."

"It certainly is a revelation to me that no-one has bothered to find out these things before," I said.

"You are mistaken. Edwin Babbitt and many of his followers, have given to the world much information in this line, but so few people have followed it. You know there are other rays, such as the violet, indigo and blue, which are astringent, nervine, soothing and anti-inflammatory. The violet is the most soothing to excited nerves, and the blue to excited blood. In cold dormant conditions, such as paralysis, blue and violet are contra-indicated."

"Do you know any good instances in which the blue or violet light had a healing effect?" I enquired.

"Yes. There was an elderly lady who for eleven years had never been entirely free from pain a single day. Her left leg was affected, and the knee, ankle and foot were swollen to twice their size. Three panes of blue glass were inserted in a west window, and the first bath was applied to the ankle, where the pain and soreness were located. It was astonishing how in only two hours the purplish colour and the lump on the ankle disappeared as well as the pain and the soreness. However, during the night the pain re-appeared in the foot and was again driven away by a light treatment. However, the most astonishing thing occurred when the knee swelled up, and she was placed in a blue glass bath, the swelling and soreness disappeared and the leg took on a normal appearance, and she was able to walk about the house. The toes of her left foot had been benumbed until she took the blue glass sun bath which restored to her her normal powers."

"That is so interesting. What else would the blue glass cure?" I asked inquisitively.

"There is a case of violent hemorrage of the lungs, there is a case of cerebro-spinal meningitis which were cured by the blue light process. There is the case of a neuralgic head-ache, general nervousness, rheumatism, a tumour on an infant, sunstroke, sciatica, nervous irritability, as well as a case of lunacy," answered my teacher.

"I should like to hear the story of the cure of sunstroke with blue."

"There was a man who suffered severely for two years from the effects of sunstroke, and by merely wearing a blue band inside of his hat, was considerably relieved. This refutes the silly idea that colour has no power except when the sun shines on it. It is true that sunlight stimulates the action of the colour, but all substances have their potencies according to their colour quite independent of light. There are other cases, of course, that could be discussed at great length," answered my companion.

"If a human being can be charged with a light, can other substances be charged with light and still retain the original effect of light?" I questioned.

"Baron Reichenbach put some water in the sunlight, and kept it there for five minutes. Then he had a sensitive drink it, and immediately he recognized that the water had been magnetised. Water which stood twenty minutes in the sunshine was found to be as strongly magnetic as water that had been charged with a large magnet. Baron Reichenbach put his hand in that of Miss Reichel, one of his sensitives, and let her get used to its vibrations. Then he went out into the sunshine, and after ten minutes, returned, and gave her the same hand. She was very much astonished at the increased force which he experienced, and the cause of which remained unknown to her. The sun had impregnated the hand much as a magnet would do."

"Wouldn't it be wonderful if we could bottle up this sun force!" I ventured.

"You can bottle up the sun-force, as you call it, by placing a bottle of water in the sun for two days, then drink a few swallows, and you will be surprised what a burning sensation it will give you. Be sure that the bottle is clear and transparent. If a person is very delicate, they should always drink sun-charged water, as they will gain a great deal of revitalizing power from it. One can use sugar of milk, or sugar and pulverized gum arabic, as they are nearly neutral, and they constitute good vehicles for the luminous forces. There is another important application of this system, and that is colour-charged air. Blue light is one of the great antiseptics of the world. It will bring about a new era in the treatment of pulmonary consumption and tuberculosis. The International Congress of Physicians have declared that sunlight is the most practical of all antiseptics. They were probably not aware that the blue part of sunlight constitutes the leading antiseptic influence. A French physician boiled a piece of pork which was heavily infested with trichinae, and found that some of the animals were still alive. He exposed another piece of the same pork to the sun and found that they had been killed. Pasteur demonstrated that rooms that had no sunlight became overcharged with bacteria. That is the reason why close and shaded rooms have an unpleasant and musty odour."

"Now I understand why I can't stay indoors in certain rooms. They give me a chill. I should like to know more about charging sugar of milk with the blue and violet light. Will you tell me more about it?"

"Yes indeed I can. Dr. Adolf von Gerhardt of Germany charged sugar of milk with blue and violet light, and gave this to an infant who had terrible cramps, and was according to all physicians, lost. He covered the point of a knife with sugar of milk and poured it down the child's mouth. Within fifteen minutes the cramps ceased, and the child became well. The beauty of these recommendations is that they are perfectly safe and gentle in action, and enduring in character."

"Thank you for that piece of information. I shall certainly use it. But what interests me beyond anything is the great healing power of sunlight. Tell me something about that. There must certainly be some very bad effects on people that have no sunlight."

"All white light is composed of all colours. Pure sunlight vitalizes the general system, especially the skin, and in warm seasons, is particularly stimulating and healing. Tumours and colds and other diseases have been cured by sunlight. Sunlight combines both thermal and electrical rays and covers every variety of power, by exposing any part of the body to the sun for a reasonable length of time, the skin becomes darker and rosier. The carbon is driven into the skin by the light, and stimulates the nerves of the surface, and a rosy appearance is developed. This makes the outer cuticle able to resist external influences of atmosphere, and prevents taking cold. It also takes inflammation from the internal organs. If light should be cast through a glass, it becomes softer and more refined, as it is strained of some of its coarser elements. This is not desirable when a great deal of power is required. There was a lady who was very feeble and negative, and used to be allergic to colds. After taking sunbaths on the skin and over the lungs she seldom took cold. She thus fortified herself against the external atmosphere by toughening the cuticle of the skin," said my companion.

"I have always been sensitive to the lack of light, and have been made very uncomfortable in certain situations when the minimum of light was permitted to penetrate into the rooms," I ventured.

"That is not unusual," answered my companion, "as Dr. Forbes Winslow in his book entitled 'Light, its Influence on Life and Health,' says that those who live and pursue their calling in situations where the minimum of light is permitted to penetrate, suffer seriously in bodily and mental health. The total exclusion of sunbeams induces the severest forms of green sickness and chlorosis and other anaemic conditions which are dependent on impoverished and disordered states of the blood. When the eyes become bloodless, and there is a death-like pallor, and the skin seems shrunken, and there is a loss of appetite and general degeneration sets in, that person suffers from premature old age and green sickness. The cure for this would be sunlight treatments, and the patient would commence to flower and bloom and gradually regain their normal strength. Dr. Ellsworth of Hertford said that he experimented with rabbits. He took one and shut it up away from sunlight, and in a few weeks it died of consumption. It was later found that the tubercules in his lungs were as perfectly formed as in the human species, and the symptoms were exactly the same. Many people keep themselves pale through the use of parasols. These should be dispensed with, and the sailor who is ever in the pure air and sunlight should be taken as an example. Housewives should stop closing out the sun from their homes because their children will grow up sickly and dwarfed, filled with aches and pains, just because they want to preserve the carpets. Stop treating the sun as if it were an enemy, it is our glorious friend. Pliny said that for six hundred years Rome was the mightiest of nations because at that time they had terraces called solariums built on the tops of their houses, and they would take solar airbaths frequently. Florence Nightingale was a great advocate of letting sunlight into the sick-room. She said, 'where there is sun there is thought.' All physiology goes to confirm this. On the shady side of deep valleys there is cretinism. Where there are cellars and unsunned sides of narrow streets there is degeneracy and weakness of mind and body. If you put a pale withering plant and a pale withering human into the sun and they are not too far gone, each will recover their health and spirit. The lack of pure air and light in the mines shows on the health of the miners. It is interesting to note that amongst the miners it is impossible to find a man who has not got some bodily deformity or arrested physical development. Most of the affections of children are due to the deficiency of light and air. Why should not our nurseries be built of glass?" asked my companion.

"Your saying this reminds me that I seem to be starved for light, and would often suffer from chills when put into an unsunned room. Many unhappy days of my childhood were spent in this atmosphere without realising what the cause was," I said.

"If mothers only knew the value of light to the skin in childhood, especially to children of a scrofulous tendency, they would have plenty of glass-house nurseries where the children might run around and fill their skins with sun and oxygen. Leukemia is a case of exclusion of sun which produces this anaemic condition. The absence of essential elements of light alters the physical composition of the blood and seriously prostrates the vital strength and enfeebles the nervous energy, which according to Dr. Forbes Winslow, eventually induces organic changes in the heart, brain and muscular tissues."

"How do you explain the fact that some people cannot take the sun. It seems injurious to them," I anxiously asked.

"Yes, that is true. Those that indulge in alcohol, opium and other cerebral stimulants as well as they who have large active brains, filled with blood, cannot take the red of the sun, and need more the blue or violet principle as counterbalancing agents. If one wants to prevent sunstroke, when there is a tendency to a hot brain, one must wear a light-coloured well-ventilated hat with a blue lining. One should eat plenty of fruit and one should wet the hair at the temples and top of the head, but not the back of the head. A quick cure for sunstroke is shown by this illustration. There was a man lying for three hours in a coma brought on by intense heat. His friends had drawn him into the darkest corner of the room where there was the least air, and had even failed to unloosen his clothing. The cure for this condition was simple. Iced water should have been pounded over his back, legs and feet. This should also be applied to the face, temples, forehead and top of the head, but never the back of the head. Then a pail of hot water should be poured on the back of the neck, being careful not to reach as far as the back of the head. This would immediately produce remarkable results. This same hot water treatment is also good for paralysis."

"How very practical to know these things," I said. "But what are the instruments with which one can give oneself the colour healing process. All this that you have told me shows the wonderful healing power of light and colour, but I should like to know more about the material through which colour is transmitted."

"I shall be very pleased to tell you what I can on the subject. Dr. Pancoast wrote a book called "Blue and Red Light." He says that painted glass does not have the same effect as glass coloured in the process of manufacture. Cobalt blue glass is brilliant to look at, but contrary to belief instead of gaining the cooling and soothing principle of blue solely, this glass transmits every colour in the spectrum, both visible and invisible, says Edwin Babbitt. Sir John Herschel also has shown how finely the very hottest invisible rays below the red are passed through cobalt glass. It is not perfect therefore and cannot be used for inflammatory conditions, whereas a deep blue glass, coloured by cupro-sulfate of ammonia, has a deep rich colour, and is a true vehicle of colour electricity. It is completely free of thermal rays, and therefore stands at the head of all the colours for general calming and cooling of the brain when this is inflamed. Mr. Hunt, in his researches on light, describes the various styles of glass. He says glass coloured green with iron oxide is scarcely surpassed for its electrical effects. Very brilliant copper green admits violet blue and a small amount of orange, and a little yellow and a great deal of green. Violet glass (manganese) has the yellow rays nearly wanting, the red rays are shortened, and all the other rays are put into intense oval patches of blue. Red or pink glass is very beautiful. It is equivalent to gold. The red-orange glass is equivalent to silver. The pure yellow is made with carbon. Then there is the yellow made with iron which has the fine tonic effect of fine iron. Blue and violet light are the best for inducing sleep in nervous conditions. The solar Thermalume invented by Edwin Babbitt is really a solar sweat bath. It is a powerful instrument which concentrates light on the whole body at once. It places colour forces on every part of the body according to its needs, and combines sweating with a strong vitalizing agency. The chromodisc is another instrument which concentrates the rays mainly by reflection. And the chromo lens does it by refraction. Both are intended to throw great power on any part of the body, thus having very rapid action."

"Would you say," said I anxiously, "that the blue or indigo glass which are the electrical rays should be applied to inflammatory, feverish or overexcited conditions, and the red ray through the ruby glass to rouse the arterial blood, whereas the purple ray through the purple glass should animate the veinous blood of the digestive system?"

"Yes, you are perfectly right, but you have forgotten the yellow, orange and red rays through the yellow and orange glass, which awaken the nervous system, and kindle it into new action, especially in paralyzed conditions. Whereas the coprasulfate blue glass is the coolest, but when combined with an equal amount of white light or clear glass it gains a little warmth. The red-orange is the warmest of all, but when combined with white light it is made cooler. Of course, solutions of different colours, and even thin coloured drapery can be used instead of glass. This holds good for clothes as well."

"I have often wondered what would be the effect of the clothes we wear, and if their colour has anything to do with our health," I asked wonderingly.

"Did you know that white or light-coloured clothes allow more light to enter the body than those of any other colour. Black or dark-coloured clothes absorb the light and degrade it into ordinary heat. White reflects a larger amount of all the rays, but all the rays which penetrate the white garment sufficiently far pass on as white rays, while a black garment absorbs all the rays and prevents them from escaping on the other side. An example of this is that a black or a blue curtain will darken a room more than a white or a buff-coloured curtain. Dr. Franklin put various-coloured cloths on snow, the darker the colour of the cloth, the more deeply the snow melted under the solar rays. This signified that black absorbs heat more than it transmits it. It is for this reason that black clothing is more endurable in Winter than in Summer, as it absorbs the heat away from the body, as well as absorbing the sun's rays, and converts these sun's rays into heat. As a tonic for the skin, light-coloured clothing is wonderful. This has a more animating effect than dark clothing. There was a lady doctor at a Turkish bath who told Edwin Babbitt that she could always tell the ladies who had been wearing black, because of the withered appearance of their skins, and that she felt that she could cure any person of a cold by asking them to wear white clothing for two days. The skin and the nerves are made more active by the light, whereas the lungs, liver and kidneys are less burdened, and the external system becomes positive. It is best to wear white underclothes as they transmit most of the rays. Red stockings however, are excellent," volunteered my companion.

Colour in Vegetable Life.

"I think this is most interesting," said I, "and I certainly have wondered about all these things."

"There has been a great deal of vagueness on the subject of colours. You are not the only one that feels that they know so little. For thousands of years the sun has been sending its glorious power upon the world. It has been painting its lessons on all things. And yet man's eyes have not been opened to see them. But as soon as men learn the fact that the positive force lies in Nature's finer forces, and not in the coarser forces, they will be thankful to those that have led them along this path. There is also the effect of colour in vegetable life. Red develops the reproductive principle in plants. Yellow, because of its power over the nervous system, is most active in animal life. Dr. Downs and Mr. Blunt, in a paper that they read at the World's Society, showed that yellow generates animalcules most rapidly, and red came next. Blue destroys animalcules and also white light prevents their forming. Therefore it is only logical that the warm light of Summer generates insect life, while the blue light of cold weather destroys it. General Plaisanton in his work talked about a professional gardener who tried to protect his plants from various minute insects that were feeding on them. Nothing succeeded, however, but the blue ray. He built a small triangular frame like a soldier's tent, and covered it with blue gauze. He prepared a piece of ground and sowed his seeds in it. He covered this portion with the blue gauze frame, while he left the other parts exposed to the attacks of the insects. Everything outside of the frame was eaten by the insects, while the portion protected

escaped entirely. It is interesting that blue glass if introduced
into apartments, would prevent flies."

"That certainly is interesting," I said, "but: does that mean
that plants will grow better under the blue ray?"

"No, the electrical rays penetrate the soil, and cause ger-
mination. But the healthy growth of plants above the ground
requires also the thermal rays, such as the yellow, which helps
to deposit carbon from the atmosphere. The flowering and
fruitage of plants are accomplished by the red thermal rays,
whereas the heat of hot-houses and the progress of healthy
vegetable growth is increased remarkably by a small amount
of blue combined with a larger amount of clear glass. Plants
that are withered are often revived by the blue ray. Light
animates and quickens the action of plants, and shadows render
them more negative, and is favourable to oxydation. It is
strange how plants are attracted by their chemical affinities,
and repulsed by other plants near to them. Brilliantly coloured flowers are apt to have less fragrance than inconspicu-
ous or white flowers. Because the Spring time of the year is
cooler and therefore more electrical, it is better adapted to ger-
mination than the Summer. While the Summer and early
Autumn, because of the thermal rays, are better adapted for
fruition," said my companion.

I had suddenly been lifted into this wonderful world of
light and colour, and I realized that up till now I had only
been living in Nature's outer temple, and that by entering the
vestibule of the inner temple, through the unfolding of the
mysterious workings of the Odic light and colour, I had taken
my first step towards the mountain of life itself. Should I dare
to open up a door farther within than the mere realms of
physical life?

The Beauty of Nature's Finer Forces.

"Why not," said a voice. "You have been in awe of mountains, of the ocean and of the world. Why not know more of the intellect which is the spark of Infinity. I am called Psychic Colour."

"Psychic Colour! You must be finer than ordinary light or colour."

"Yes. I am about four times as fine as ordinary light and I will show you the fine interior views of Nature and her forces. I will show you that there are Universes within Universes—Worlds within Worlds—and that the condition of things which we inhabit is not the real universe. It is merely a shadow. While the real Cosmos is more intense and powerful. It can be compared to a mist with a solid substance. Yet there are people that think that the lower universe is all, while the sublimer realms of existence are to be wasted. Intellect is the combination of power, but may be affected indirectly by ordinary light, by Odic light, and mostly by psychic light. Psychic lights and colours are beautiful beyond expression, and manifest the infinite activities of Nature unseen by ordinary eyes. This higher vision shows that there is a grander universe within the visible, which is the true Cosmos. There are thousands of people that can see these psychic colours which reveal the primary laws of force. Scientists should not only dwell on the coarser grades of matter, which are but the outer shell of things, they should endeavour to find the richer kernels within."

"Are there many people who can see these higher colours?" I asked.

"Yes, there are thousands of persons who are able to see finer grades of colour. Some can see them with their eyes wide open in broad daylight. According to Edwin Babbitt, there was a woman called Minnie Merton who had always seen colours emanating from people ever since childhood. And she could read character from these emanations. There was a well-known judge who could often tell the general character of a speaker's thoughts before they were even spoken, from the colours of the emanations around his head. There are many people who can see colours around persons and objects, but they don't know their meaning."

Light Renders Opaque Substances Transparent.

"Is that why there are people that are clear-seeing or clair-voyant?"

"Only those who can get 'en rapport' with the finer light are considered clairvoyant or clear-seeing. Sensitives who have seen Odic light making bodies transparent, are not the same as those who can see the still finer psychic light. I have seen two men with their eyes shut distinguish objects placed before them. They could tell the colour and value of cards. Major Buckley, according to Edwin Babbitt, developed the ability to read writing which had been hidden away in nuts or boxes carried by eighty-nine people. The longest motto read contained ninety-eight words. One of Major Buckley's clair-voyantes read one hundred and three mottoes. Duke University is doing a fine job in making these finer sensibilities more known to the world. Dr. Rhine, in his book 'The Reach of the Mind' shows countless cases and experiments. Then there is the Society for Psychical Research and Enlightenment which is based on the work of Edgar Casey who was one of the greatest clairvoyants the world has ever had. He was a famous som-nambulist."

"What is a somnambulist? Can you explain that to me?"

"Why, yes," answered my teacher, "ordinary sleep is caused by drawing the vital ethers as well as the blood away from the front of the brain, and into the cerebellum. This leaves the mental powers so inactive that they appear to be unconscious. Whereas magnetic sleep, or somniscience, brings into action the finer interior forces. These interior forces are quicker and more penetrating than the coarser vital ethers. Therefore, they cause greater keenness of mental power. When these forces are sufficiently developed, it is called clairvoyance."

"How can one induce this condition?" I asked curiously.

"This condition is induced by fastening the mind on some object which can either be near or at a distance. Thus the finer ethers are drawn outward, and if one wants to assist the coarser ethers away from the brain, one must make downward passes over the body," said my teacher very informatively.

"Can you give me any examples that will assist me in understanding better this lucid magnetic sleep?"

"Dr. William B. Carpenter said that although the brain has not ordinarily more than one fortieth of the weight of the body, yet it is estimated to receive one fifth to one sixth of the whole circulatory blood. He also said that the four arterial trunks which convey blood into the skull, three may be tied, and still have consciousness remain. But if the fourth is tied unconsciousness takes place. Often people are asphyxiated with depraved blood which has too much carbon in it. But people of great will power can fire up the vital force by the finest psychic principle, and so animate the blood as to prevent many disasters even though the blood is impure. There are various kinds of sleep. If the animating ether is drawn to the back of the brain, and to the body, leaving the front of the brain inactive, a quiet condition of sleep is induced. If a greater quantity of blood and finer ethers is drawn downwards, a dreamy kind of sleep ensues. And if still a greater quantity of blood is drawn, a perfect unconscious sleep is produced. During this quiet time of the brain, the rest of the system is doubly active, building up its cells and tissues to make up for what has been destroyed during the waking hours."

"I still don't understand if ordinary sleep stupefies and renders the mind a blank, how can magnetic sleep open up new and wonderful powers of intelligence?"

"That is a very good question, and quite a deep one. When we abstract the coarser forces from the brain, and bring into action the refined powerful psychic ethers, it is bringing one nearer to the finer forces. It is just the same as in the case of Baron Reichenbach's sensitives where they took the ordinary light from the room, in order that the Odic light might be more easily seen. The gray matter of the brain is the immediate seat of ordinary sensation and mental action, while the more interior forces are quickened by the chemical affinities of the inner surface of the reddish-gray matter and the outer layer of the interior bluish-white matter. When these are called outward they produce a much better mental action than the slower coarser forces of grey matter which are usually predominant. Now, if these forces are called outward and put into great action, the entire brain is filled with a diviner light. This blends with the same grade of diviner light of the external world, and produces higher vision. In other words, the rays of light fall on the retina of the eye where they leave their imprint. This imprint or image is carried to the external sensorium by a certain grade of vital electricity that is just suited for it, and thus we get the wonderful effect of vision. The Bell telephone works in the same manner. First, the waves of sound strike an artificial diaphragm at one end of the line, they are then transferred by means of electricity through a wire to another diaphragm and human ear at the other end. In human sight the first diaphragm is equivalent to the retina at the back of the eye. The electrical wire is the optic nerve, and the second diaphragm, or receiver, is the interior surface of the reddish-grey matter of the brain. And the ear of the listener is represented by the human spirit. In magnetic conditions, the eyes might be wide open, but the ordinary light cannot make any impression, as the internal vital electricity is withdrawn to other parts of the body. But the fine psychic ethers which have full play, receive the finer light that emanates from all substances, and carries to the inner sensorium, which has its culminating point at the junction of the grey and white matter of the brain. The mind thus receives the most exquisite images, and higher vision is attained. By means of ordinary light, one may see through transparent bodies, because the light penetrates them. But by means of psychic light, the vision may pass through nearly all things as easily as ordinary vision passes through glass."

"Must one have this magnetic sleep in order to have this finer vision?" I asked.

"No, it is not necessary to get into magnetic sleep to have this finer vision. There are many who can cause the finer ethers of the brain to gain the ascendancy over the coarser ethers, so as to be able to see immediately without closing their eyes. There are others that are able to throw the animal forces away from their front brain through sheer will power. This they do by throwing their eye-balls upward and back as in a sleeping condition. There are again others who are less developed who will have to look at some object in front of or above them, or think of some place far away, in order to draw the psychic forces sufficiently outward," volunteered my companion.

"Thank you," said I, "that is very clear. But I should like to know more on how to develop this finer vision. I now understand how this force is possible."

"Because of the fineness of these ethers which are so swift and powerful, it is quite an achievement to learn how to use them. The first thing to do is to have a person who is already well-charged with these finer forces, and is himself a clairvoyant, make passes over the head downward especially over the eyes and forehead, and thus transfer his own power to the subject. These passes should be made one to two inches from the body, from the head to the foot. This, Dr. Braid of England, styled as hypnotism. His method consisted of having his subjects look steadily at an object placed in front and slightly above them for some time, while downward passes were made. But one of the most practical methods is that of sitting in a reclining position with the back to the north or north-east, with but a dim light, and close the eyes turning the eye-balls a little upwards if possible. Hold this position if there is no pain, and then steadily and easily make an effort to see. This should be practised for about half an hour, while doing so the thought must not be allowed to wander, and the constant aim should be to see if lights, colours and forms appear. If colours don't appear in a few days, the prospect of clairvoyance is very small," answered my teacher.

"Is there no way for everyone to acquire this gift?" I asked, thinking of the many that might not be able to see.

"Yes, Dr. Fahnestock has developed a system of artificial somnambulism. He calls it statuvolnece. He has developed this method remarkably well, and has effected many cures on the mental system through this method. In order to quote him, he says: When persons are desirous of entering this state, I place them on a chair where they may be at perfect ease. I then request them to close their eyes at once and remain perfectly calm. They are next instructed to throw their mind to some familiar place. They are asked to keep their mind on this familiar place or object for some time. When they seem to tire of one thing, or they don't see anything, they are directed to others, until clairvoyance is induced. When this has been effected, the rest of the senses fall in at once, but if the subject's interest or attention is divided there is difficulty in entering into this state. Very often, the subject feels that he is falling away or floating off. But there is no cause for alarm. If he is very intensely concentrated on a place or an object, he will begin to feel that he is there in person, and to see what is going on and hear the words that are spoken, even though they are hundreds of miles away. He might even know the thoughts of the people there. While in this state the subject, at the request of the operator, can use these forces with wonderful power. He can will a certain disease to depart, and it will often leave. He can determine to be strong, and self-controlled after awaking from this condition. He will then find himself in possession of a new strength. He can will to have any part of his body become senseless. After a little practice, he can do this in a few minutes and become master of himself. This can be used advantageously when having a tooth pulled. If done correctly no sensations will be felt in the jaw, thus signifying that this mighty psychic force, under the brain, can hold the sensory nerves entirely in check. There was the case of a lady who could describe what was going on in her home in another state. She said she was not quite sure whether she saw her people or whether it was her imagination. But on writing home, she found she was exactly correct."

"Tell me of some of the instances in which these psychic forces can bless mankind."

"First of all, psychic forces bring into action a sublimer vision. This vision reveals both the wonders of the interior and exterior universe. There is no instrument invented that has this power. It cannot be produced by the telescope or the microscope. This power reveals the realm of the intellect, and that finer radiance which can't be seen in the external world. When this power is more developed, there will be less mistakes of vision, and discoveries in psychological and physiological phenomena of great importance will take place. Another blessing is that besides the sublimer vision of the possibilities of the universe and of human life, there is the possibility of the control of physical, mental and moral diseases. Because through the mental forces, one is able to build up and heal the physical system. There are many magnetic healers who have cured multitudes by the touch of their hand, and many times without even touching their subjects. This was done while they were in normal conditions, and by a powerful effort of their will. It was found that downward passes over the body sooths and quiets excited nerves, whereas upward passes arouse dormant and cold portions of the body. Zouave Jacob, of France, was a wonderful magnetic healer, and cured multitudes," said my teacher.

"Can this force also be applied to mental and moral conditions, as well as physical?" I asked.

"Yes indeed. The psychic forces of different parts of the brain have been charged and regulated, and their equivalent negative poles in the body have been made to abstain from liquor, animal passions, and to stimulate much greater activity in the mental and moral forces. For instance a little girl, six years old, was able to change the complete nature of a burly sea-tyrant, her uncle, who was one of the roughest men that ever trod a deck. Yet this child was able to render him helpless by repeatedly manipulating his head while he held her in his lap. She had witnessed a few experiments and believed she could do the same, and so she tried, and accomplished the greatest miracle, as he turned into a gentle man. The finer forces combined with the gentler pure element of his little magnetiser, were made to penetrate and refine the region of his external brain. Often, the face of the person in the highest stages of magnetic sleep, becomes irradiated, and heavenly beyond expression. There are many people that have started nobler and truer lives because of the development of these higher elements. Because there are some fortune tellers who convert their ability to a low end does not argue against the holier purposes to which these forces might be consecrated. The development of these forces begets a keenness of vision in mental perception which, when highly developed, will penetrate fraud and hypocrisy, thus destroying their practice. People have traced jewelry and have found a great number of stolen objects through this superior vision. Cases of epilepsy, rheumatism, hysteria, fevers and all diseases have been cured. Another marvelous thing about psychic control is, that fear which lets the animal forces rush to the brain and confuse the intellect, can be kept in check by these means. Hundreds of lives lost from panic and fear, might have been saved. Dr. Williams, a psychologist, offered a prize of ten thousand dollars to anyone who would remain quiet every morning for a year, and use his will-power for twenty minutes before arising, if at the end of that time he did not admit that he had not received vast advantages from this practice. A gentleman tried this and gained such additional power of mind and body, that he refused to take the ten thousand dollars. This will power should be used in throwing the life forces to all parts of the body, and in determining to be calm, gentle and self-possessed through the day, regardless of what excitement might occur," said my good companion.

"Do the Odic colours and force work in the body at all?"

"Yes, psychic colours vary in different parts of the brain. Dr. J. R. Buchanan, professor in various medical colleges, and a cerebral psychologist, said that one way in which he gained his knowledge was by consulting his finer vision, and by charging with finer ethers his finger tips, then touching various parts of the brains of sensitive people, each portion having its own peculiar manifestations. This he did in the presence of witnesses and friends. First he touched the organ of self-esteem in a lady. Immediately, the active vital fluid communicated, worked, and she began to claim women's rights. When he touched the organ of humility, she immediately changed her tone, and proclaimed that she was a weak woman after all. The poet Bryant was touched on his ideality, and thereby his own ideality became so ignited that he burst into glowing language. These facts show that different parts of the brain have their own special mental and emotional characteristics, that they get their vitality and activity from the psychic aura which passes through them. Much of the character and conduct of humans come from the conditions of the brain, which, because of their ignorance, they do not know how to control. Only when they become acquainted with the psychic lights and forces through which they move, will they be able to correct and control perverted conditions by reaching at their cause. A fine example of what can be done is the instance of a patient cured of alcoholic stimulus. Edwin Babbitt effected this cure himself. His method was to draw the hot forces of the back of the brain by passing the hands over the part and down the arms to the hands. In the case of the alcoholic, he drew the heat away from the portion directly in front of the ears, and by scattering in different directions the heat of the epigastrium, and thus cooling the inflamed gastric membrane which is the cause of the burning thirst for liquors. A person of stupid perceptions can become quickened by animating the region over the eyebrows. This is done by passes of the hand each day. His reasoning powers can become quickened by holding the hands over the forehead."

"That is wonderful," I replied. "I can see now how these psychic forces can bless mankind by opening up a sublimer vision of possibilities, and also by selfpsychology, which is a condition brought about by getting 'en rapport' with the psychic forces. Thus by the power of the will, the subject can cause all sensation to leave any part of the body thus correcting any mental deficiency."

"That is very good. I am very glad that I have made myself that much understood. That is right, every part of the intellectual, moral or passionate nature of man can be aroused into greater action by charging different portions of the brain and body with these psychic forces. This is done by means of the hands, and is known as magnetic healing. When the subject is in a somnambulic state, each part of the brain is aroused in a special and intense kind of thought and feeling, which is entirely different from every other part, showing that the brain has its own special organs or regions of mental characteristics. The inspired Plato well understood the basis of mental action. He said: 'It is not art which makes thee excel but a divine power which moves thee, such as in the stone which Eurypides named the magnet, and some the Herculean stone which attracts the iron rings.' The psychic colours which vary in different parts of the brain, are in close harmony with these organs."

"Has the brain got colour radiations too?"

"Yes, the fine forces of the brain radiate colours just as the Odic forces are found in nature. The left hemisphere of the brain receives the blue and electrical forces, but radiates the warm forces stronger than the right hemisphere of the brain. While the right hemisphere of the brain radiates blue forces and receives the red more strongly. The left brain is stronger in the domain of intellect, while the right is stronger in that of organic life."

"Is that what is meant by intuition?" I asked curiously.

"No, intuition is in the same proportion as the psychic forces are in a person. Geniuses are proteges of swiftness in mental action. They are bound in these fine ethers. Woman is much more intuitive than man on an average, thus more sensitive to the influx of the finer ethers. Systems that are psychically strong have tremendous recuperative faculty. Intuition is the direct use of the fine and swift ethers, by means of which our thoughts can move on the wings of lightning. This is woman's favourite method. She can bring herself into 'rapport' with these finer ethers quicker than man."

"But what are the colours of these ethers," I asked.

"The poles of the bodily organs radiate colours which form a chemical affinity with the brain. You see, the positive poles of the human battery are in the brain, and the negative poles in the body. It has been found that the lungs are orange and red and some yellow. Edwin Babbitt saw these colours and said that the stomach has as its ruling colour yellow, with a sufficient of blue to give it a yellow-green cast. The sexual organs are surrounded by reddish brown. Thus the front and upper head match the front and upper body. The lungs constitute a chemical affinity with the forehead and bridge of the nose which connects with the breathing apparatus. Amativeness with its red elements corresponds with the bluish portion of the lower spine. The heart, according to Mrs. Somerby, a great sensitive, is a dark red, the bowels are yellow with the lowest part greenish mixed with red. The back lower brain is a dark red which merges gradually into bluish white as it reaches the spine. The spine is a bluish white turning to reddish brown at the lower end, while the whole nervous system streams forth bluish white light just as the arteries exhibit currents of red light. The solar plexus radiates the entire rainbow. The feet send out red and all the warm colours and head blue or cold colours."

"Are there any particular colours that make the psychic ethers act?"

"Yes, the reddish grey-matter of the brain and the bluish-white matter of the nerves constitute the elements of chemical affinity without which the psychic ethers could not act and hence all sensation would cease."

"Thank you very much for all this information. I now realize that we have a finer body within a coarser body, and these are composed of materials which are never known to decay. I have now had the advantage of having natural law unfolded to me, and I realize the great masterpiece of God's great handiwork. In my search for the secret of power I have learned as Socrates says, that the inner man can only be found by 'knowing thyself.' I also am in agreement with Marcus Aurelius, the wisest man in Italy whose formula for growth and power was 'control thyself.' You have given me the information how to do this, whereas the Man from Galilee, who tapped the universe with the statement of 'Deny thyself' has taught me the secret of that power through nature's finer forces. In other words the kernel of all the laws of growth are found in these statements given to me, and I can only irrigate the garden of my ideas with the light that you have given me, and I shall use the strings of the Muse's harp and try to unite the source of all power as shown to me by nature and light."

My dear Reader, since you have been so kind as to journey with me through the rainbow, I hope that this journey to the land of light has revealed to you, as well as to me, that all of our troubles and sins are caused by the lack of understanding of nature's finer forces. Most people face life losing the little original contact they had with nature when young, so that they act like unfocused opera glasses. The only way to keep in focus is to read the bible of light, and interpret nature in our everyday living.

CONCLUSION

Color has thrilled and fascinated human beings since the beginning of time. In the early days, the deepest mysteries of life in the universe were closely associated with it. Man looked upon color as the emanation of spiritual rays of a great power, —God. In the study of the aura they found a mark of spiritual and mental development, and as the studies of human life increased, they saw color in spirit, breath and soul.

Today, with all our new systems and teachings, the world turns with renewed interest to the study of light and the spectrum. People sense and give the required recognition to its strange influence. They instinctively know that color controls the emotions, thus influencing human moods. The greatest need of mankind, today, is to learn and to recognize the language of the emotions. Since most of our city nerves and office jitters come from a lack of knowledge of this delicate and subtle field, the reactions to color environment are so significant that they suggest the key to human nature and provide a very strong clue to personality analysis.

A. K

RAINBOW COLORS

I love to paint my shutters blue,
 My pillars rose, my gables green,
My doors a bright vermillion hue,
 With orange frescoes in between,
And then to hear the bigwigs say,
 "How crude! All houses should be gray!"
And when I've tinted vacant spots
 Of walls in some delightful tones
With gallant swirls and polka dots
 And when the solemn pedants groan,
"This really isn't done, you know!"
 I ask, "Why not? I like it so."
Must all the world be dark as doom,
 Poor hoodman-blind—for such you be?
Behold, against your timid gloom
 In laughing hues of life and glee
Our radiant rainbow! Let me think;
 We'll make that chimney salmon-pink!

ERNEST J. STEVENS

INDEX

INDEX

Glossary

GLOSSARY OF COLOR TERMINOLOGY FOR THOSE IN THE ART WORLD

Plato said that knowledge depends on the definition of the general term. Thus, a color vocabulary is herewith listed. Become acquainted with these definitions in the expression of color language.

Achromatic: Colorless, or lacking in color.

Advancing Colors: Colors giving the illusion of nearness to the spectator. Red-orange is warm, therefore advancing and stimulating to the sensations.

Analogous Colors: Colors so closely related that they can be mistaken for each other. Some examples are blue, blue-green and green.

Aniline Colors: Those produced from coal-tar products.

Atmospheric: Colors, such as sky-blue, which give an impression of space and air.

Binder: The cohesive liquid in paint that acts to bind the ingredients. Linseed and poppy oils are binders employed in oil painting.

Blending: The method of merging two pigments so that their colors intermingle.

Bloom: A clouded finish often found on varnished surfaces. Similar to that existent on fruits such as the plum and grape.

Bright: Term applied to vivid, intense colors, such as orange or sunflower yellow. The opposite of dull and dark.

Brilliant: A greater degree of brightness.

Broken Color: The interspersing of one color with another by means of short strokes so that an impression of airiness is created.

Cast: The tendency or inclination of one color towards another. For example, the pale yellow of sulphur has a greenish cast.

Center of Interest: The dominant center which gains attention through color, while other details are subservient to it. The focal point of interest in a painting on display.

Chroma: An intense purity and strength of undiluted colors, not neutralized, and free from white or grey.

Colors: The sensation of hues, tints and shades produced through the rejection of light by the retina of the eye.

Coloring Strength: The relative strength of pigments in coloring a light base.

Compatability: The ability of colors to exist together without harmful reaction.

Complementary Colors: Two opposite hues which furnish completeness to each other A mixture of two primary colors results in the complement of the remaining primary.

Cool Colors: The blue colors.

Cyanic Colors: Blue colors that are dark, low in value and shading towards black. The opposite of light. In flowers, beginning with blue and running through violet and purple to red. (Delphiniums. Forget-me-nots, and Corn Flowers.)

Deep: No presence of black (ultramarine blue).

Diffused Light: Light scattered or dispersed in an even degree through ground glass.

Dominant Color: A key color which stands out.

Double Split Complementaries: Two neighboring colors of one primary combined with two neighboring colors of another.

Drier: Chemicals, such as litharge, manganese, red lead and cobalt oxide, added to paint to hasten drying.

Dull: A grey or neutral quality present in some colors, such as dusty pink.

Element: The cobalt, cadmium, copper, zinc. carbon, lead, or sulphur base of decorators' pigments.

Fixative: A thinned varnish which is applied to charcoal and pastel drawings in order to fix the colors and prevent them from coming off.

Fugitive Colors: Fading pigments.

Full Color: Great purity, strength and intensity.

Glazing: The process of applying a thin coating of raw sienna, burnt sienna. veridian green, or blanc de loque over a painted surface in order to tone down the effect of the colors already present.

Greyish: Lacking purity of color. Neutral.

Ground: The surface on which a picture is rendered.

Hue: Color. The term used to distinguish one color from another.

Impasto: The technique of applying paint thickly by means of a knife, thereby causing the paint to stand out in relief.

Inert Pigment: An inorganic chemical compound having no opalescence or glitter. Used mainly as stain.

Intense: Vivid, strong, full colors.

Irradiation: An optical illusion in which bright objects against dark backgrounds tend to appear larger than they actually are.

Isomeric Colors: Those colors which appear identical but contain different chemical or physical properties.

Juxtaposition: The placement of colors close together or side by side. From the Latin word "juxto," meaning next to.

Key, Keyed: Terminology applied to the color value of paintings. The key color is the dominant color. Dull or dark values create a low key, light or bright values a high key.

Lake: Lake colors are generally transparent. Slow in drying, they make good glazing pigment. This pigment is produced by combining coloring material with an inert base, such as alumina, blace, fixe, or whiling.

Medium: A liquid binder, or vehicle, such as linseed oil, giving fluency to pigments.

Medium Value: An in-between vale of a color. English term—"Middle Value."

Millimicron: A unit of measurement used to determine different wave lengths of spectral color. For example, green in the spectrum has a wave length of 533 to 505 millimicrons.

Monochromatic: Having but one color. A gradation in the shades of one color.

Neutral: Indeterminate color which is dull or greyed.

Neutralizing Harmony: The addition of grey to two or more colors in order to create certainties, attain subtle harmony and cause the colors to recede. Produced by an admixture of complementary colors.

Opaque: Not permitting light to pass through.

Organic Colors: Pigments of animal and vegetable dyestuff origin.

Paint Out: A sample of color applied to a surface.

Pale: Light value of color.

Palette: A selection or artists' pigments.

Pattern: The aesthetic arrangement of areas into a design.

Permanence: The changeless quality of pigments.

Permanent: Having permanence.

Pigment: Any coloring material of animal, vegetable or mineral origin. From the Latin term "Pigmentum," meaning paint.

Prism: A transparent glass optical instrument in triangular form. When sunlight passes through a prism the rays are bent twice, separating into the solar spectrum.

Receding Colors: Those which give an illusion of distance.

Refractive Index: The ratio of speed of light in air in ratio to the speed of light in another substance. Dark surfaces absorb light, light surfaces reflect light, while transparent surfaces bend or reflect light.

Saturation: The intensity or purity of color.

Secondary Colors: A combination of two primary colors in equal proportions.

Sensation: The perception of color by the mind after the original reception by the eyes.

Sheen: A faint luster, as if caused by refraction.

Siccative: Drier. From the Latin word "siccare," meaning to dry.

Simultaneous Contrast: An optical effect in which one color is influenced in hue by an adjacent color.

Spectral Colors: Those colors produced when a ray of the sun is bent by a prism.

Spectrum: Prismatic colors caused by a beam of light being broken up. The wave length of each color is separated, forming a series of hues—red-orange at one end, orange, yellow, green, blue and violet at the other. Nature's rainbow consists of these colors.

Strong: Full, intense colors.

Study: Practice reproductions utilized by students.

Surface Colors: The outer color of material objects.

Technique: The method of handling materials employed by an artist.

Texture: The effect gained through methods of material application plus the peculiar character of the surface employed.

Thumbnail Sketch: A miniature drawing.

Tincture: A tinge of color.

Tinge: A slight trace of color.

Tint: A pale or light value of color.

Tone: An intermediate hue used to reduce or subdue the intensity of a color.

Toner: Pure dyestuff in concentrated form which tones or colors.

Transparent: That permitting light to pass through.

Triadic Colors: Three colors forming an equilateral triangle.

Undertone: A color on which other colors are imposed.

Value: Term used to distinguish light colors from dark. The gradation of the shades of a color.

Vehicle: The liquid medium which forms a binder in paint (linseed oil, etc.)

Vibration: An oscillation or rapid motion. Everything in the universe has a specific rate of vibration. This rate is known as frequency.

Vignette: A form of painting in which the subject is shaded bit by bit.

Viord: Bright, intense.

Volatile Thinner: A liquid used to dilute paint. Alcohol and thin shellac are volatile thinners.

Volume Color: The color appearance of liquids.

Warm Colors: Colors in which red or yellow predominate. The fact that these colors produce a sensation of warmth can be demonstrated by the use of a sensitive thermometer. These colors are associated in our minds with heat, sun and fire.

Wash: A thin mixture of water color with water.

Wave Length: The distances between the vibrations of light that produce visible colors. Red-orange possesses the longest wave length, while violet has the shortest. Wave lengths longer than red are called infra-red, those shorter than violet are termed ultra-violet.

Yanthic Colors: Colors in which yellow predominates. Sunflowers, Buttercups, Dandelions, Marigolds, and Jonquils are flowers possessing yanthic colors.

WHO'S WHO IN THE BOOK

Walter Russell: Artist and sculptor, painter of children's portraits, painted portraits of President Theodore Roosevelt's children. Painted the Allegory called "The Might of the Ages" which was exhibited at the Turin Exhibition, also sculptured Mark Twain's Memorial in Hannibal, Mo., sculptured the John Phillip Sousa Memorial for Washington, D. C., The Charles Goodyear Memorial for Akron, Ohio, and The Joan of Arc for presentation to France. His busts are well known, such as the War President of Roosevelt, Mark Twain for London. He erected the Four Freedoms as a tribute to the American soldier. He maintains scientific research laboratories for scientific research mainly in electrical and chemical studies. President Emeritus of the Society of Arts and Sciences, Member of Academy of Fine Arts and Literature as well as Numismatic Society. Author of Genero Radioactive Concept, The Russell Chart of Elements, The Age of Innocence, The Bending Twig. Maintains a studio in New York at Carnegie Hall. Born in Boston May 19, 1871. Graduate of the Normal Art School in Boston, Museum of Fine Arts, Drexel Institute in Philadelphia, Academy Julian in Paris. Private pupil of Harry Munsell and Jean Paul Laurens.

Max Weber: Born in Byelosok, Russia, April 18, 1881. Brought by parents to America in 1891. Attended high school in Brooklyn in 1898 and the Pratt Institute in 1900. Became teacher in painting at the Art Students League in 1920. Works are found in New York Art Gallery, Gallery of Living Art in Los Angeles, Metropolitan Museum of Art in New York, Museum of Modern Art, New York, the Whitney Museum. Won the American Palmer gold medal and the Pennsylvania Academy of Fine Arts medal, the Clark Bronze medal and $1000, the Ada Garrett prize of $750, medals from the Art Institute of Chicago, Memorial American Painters. Author of Cubist Poems 1914, Essay on Art 1916, Primitives 1927. Lives in Great Neck, Long Island.

Ernest J. Stevens, M. Sc., PhD., MA.: Author of Vibrations, Their Principles; Light, Tones and Color, Their Uses, Breath Power, Natures Finer Forces. Maintained research laboratories in San Francisco.

Dr. Edward J. Babbitt: Great educator, instructor, lecturer and research writer and visioned pioneer of 25 years. Author of Principles of Light, Tone and Color, result of over 50 years of research.

Jules Guerin: Awarded Yerkers prize medal, the silver medal at the St. Louis Exposition in 1915. Director of color and decorations for Lincoln Memorial Building, Washington. Directed the decorations in the Federal Reserve Bank in San Francisco, also did the decorations in some of the biggest building. Member of many societies such as Beaux Arts Society, American Institute of Architects, Society of American Illustrators, etc.

Hogarth: English artist.
Baron Reichenbach: Austrian scientist.
Berzillius: Eminent chemist from Stockholm.
Dr. Elliotson: President, Royal Chirurgian Society of London.
Dr. Gregory: Of Edinburgh College, Scotland.
Madame Kienesberger: A sensitive used in Baron Reichenbach's experiments.
Johann Klaiber: Also a sensitive of the Reichenbach experiments.
Mr. Firke: Another sensitive.
Madame Zinkel: Another sensitive.
Dr. Forbs Winslow: Author of Influence of Light.
Nowotny: A sensative of Reichenbach experiments.
M. Baumgarten: Physics professor.